How to Make architectural models

How to

Make architectural models

Tony Renoir

Studio Vista London

Acknowledgments

Photographs are by Gordon Metcalfe

Printed in England by The Shenval Press, London and Harlow

Published in Great Britain in 1973
by Studio Vista Publishers
Blue Star House, Highgate Hill, London N19

ISBN 0 289 70371 9

Contents

Introduction

This book contains complete instructions for making models of five very different types of house. All of them are made with the same simple materials and tools which you will find listed on the next two pages.

The models can be made just as easily on a table at home as on a school desk or workbench.

Measurements are given in centimetres and inches. The two sets of measurements are not interchangeable.

On pages 16–17 you will find a colour mixing chart which will help you obtain the correct colouring for stone, brick, wood, etc, for all the models, and on page 63 there are ideas for making model trees, hedges and other garden and landscape details which will make your models more realistic.

When you have completed two or three of the models in the book you might like to try and make a model of your own design – your own home, or a famous or beautiful house or castle you have visited or seen in a book. Advice on how to start your own model is given at the end of the book.

Some of the technical architectural terms are printed in italics the first time they are used. These words are explained in the glossary on page 67.

Materials

white cardboard	Stationers and suppliers of artists' materials sell large sheets of plain white cardboard for mounting pictures.
white drawing paper	For planning out your building in rough. If you are building a model of your own design you will need to try out the model in paper first to find out if it will work properly. Paper is sometimes better to use than cardboard for very small details.
thin white paper	Pillars, chimney pots and other cylindrical parts of models can be made by winding thin paper round old pencils or drinking straws until the thickness is right.
balsa wood	You can buy lengths of balsa wood in various thicknesses, either flat or square in section. 5mm ($\frac{1}{4}$in) is the size most often used in this book.
hardboard for bases	As a base for your models you need something thicker and stronger than cardboard. Plywood or thick card would do, but hardboard is cheap and easy to cut with an ordinary saw.
cellophane	For windows, and water for ponds and moats. Buy a sheet or roll of the (non-adhesive) type used for covering library books. This is strong and will not shrink or crinkle.

Tools

a hard pencil	Use HB or harder. Keep it sharp for accurate marking out of plans and parts of building on cardboard.
a ruler	For both ruling and measurement. Do not use it for guiding knives unless it is metal.
scissors	You need a large pair for most of the straight cutting of both cardboard and cellophane.
Stanley knife or craft knife	A sharp penknife would do, but a Stanley knife is easier to hold and control. This is essential for cutting out doors, windows and any part which it is difficult to reach with scissors. NB. Place a piece of scrap cardboard under the card you are cutting to protect the table or desk top and prevent the knife point from getting blunt.
P.V.A. adhesive	Spread it thinly and evenly for all cardboard and hardboard flaps and joints.
balsa cement	Use this or any clear glue (Uhu) for gluing balsa wood and cellophane.
paints	See colour mixing chart on page 16.
brushes	Water colour brushes. A large one for roofs, roads, lawns and other flat areas – a very fine one for door and window frames, chimneys, etc.
compasses	for measuring and for sloping roofs.

Roman villa

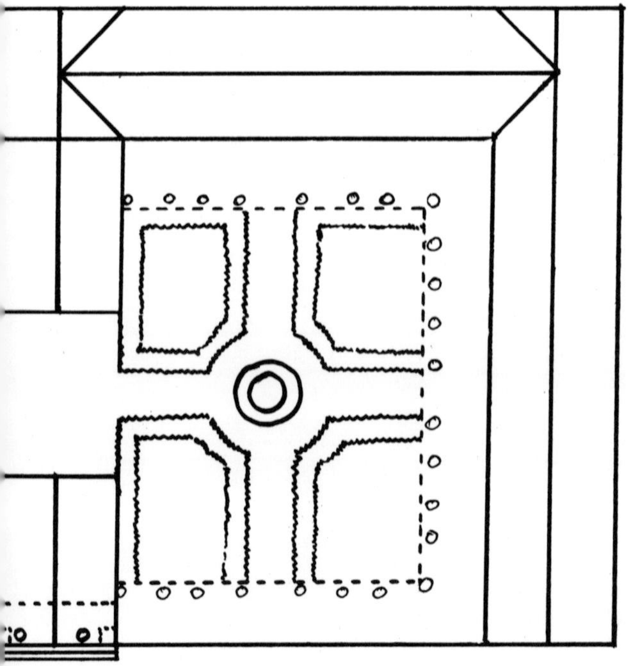

Plan looking down on the roof of the villa

The Romans built homes of similar design all over Europe. This model is based on a villa in the Romano-British city of Silchester.

The villa is built round a courtyard garden. The plan of the model is exactly 30×30cm (12×12in) square. See plan above and colour sketch on page 17.

Cut a base board (see page 7) larger than the square plan all round and mark out the square only.

On a sheet of white cardboard rule a base line 1cm ($\frac{1}{2}$in) above the lower long edge of the card.

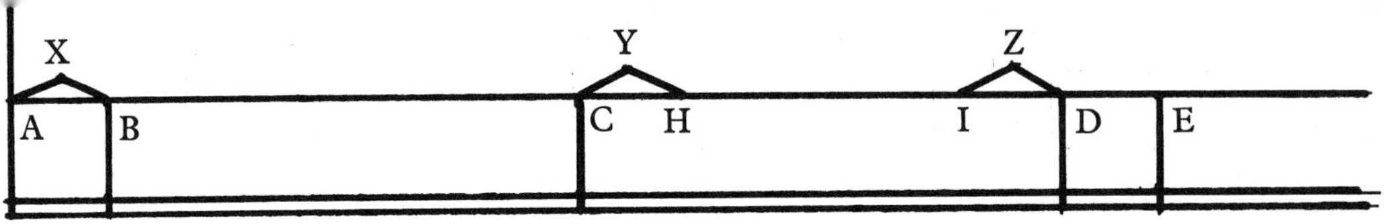

Rule a second line 6cm (2½in) above the base line. Starting from the left, measure AB 6cm (2½in), BC 30cm (12in), CD 30cm (12in), DE 6cm (2½in) on both lines.

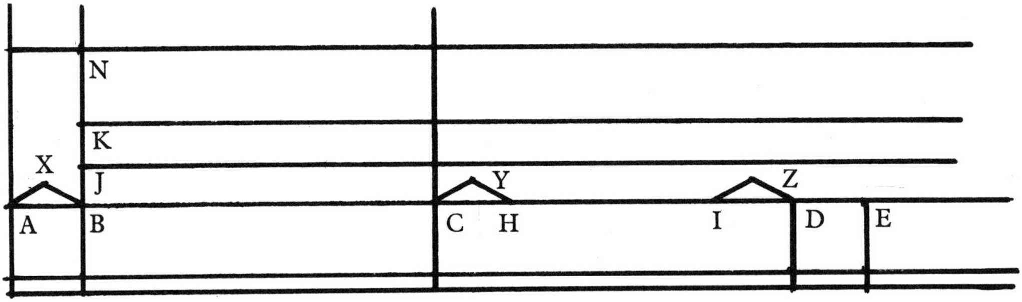

Along the top line, mark off CH and ID 6cm (2½in). For the angle of roof, put a compass point at A, B, C, H, I and D and strike arcs of 4cm (1½in). They will cross at points X, Y and Z. Draw the angles AXB, CYH and IZD.

Continue vertical lines upwards at B and C. Measure off the two roof slopes BJ and JK 4cm (1½in), then KN 6cm (2½in) for the inside wall. Carry these three measurements horizontally across the card to above E.

Draw vertical lines up from H, I, D and E. Measure off O, P, Q and E2. Draw ORH (R is the crossing of diagonals MH and OC). Mark out MS and ST 6cm (2½in) each. Mark out triangle PQU – the same as IDZ. Join UZ. Mark V, half-way between D1 and E1, and join it to Q and E2.

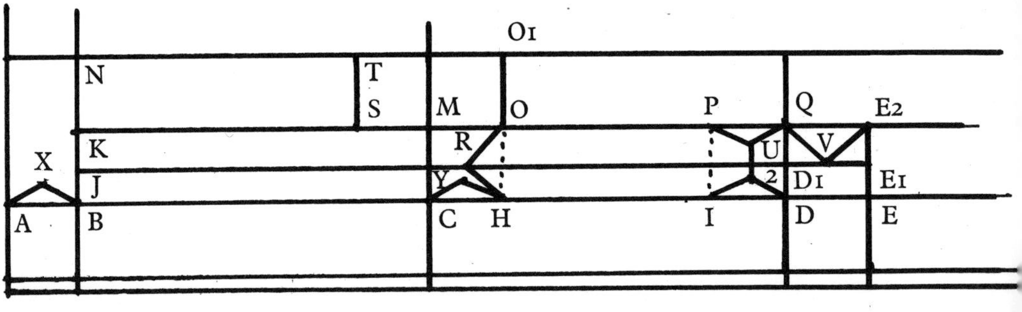

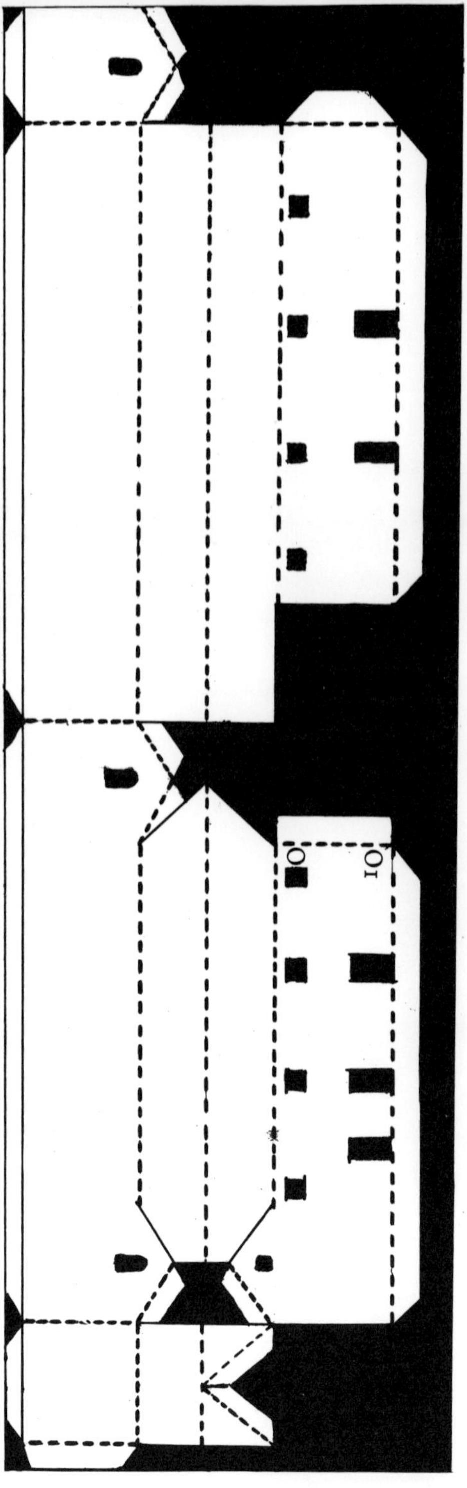

Add flaps as indicated in the left hand diagram. Mark out doors and windows. Keep all their heights the same – otherwise exact measurements are not important.

Cut away all areas shaded black in the diagram, including the doors and windows.

Score gently all dotted lines. Do this with the point of your scissors or a Stanley knife held against a metal ruler. NB. The line between 0 and 01 should be scored on the back.

The whole of the main building which forms two sides of the square can now be folded and glued. Spread glue on the flaps one at a time and stick them inside the model.

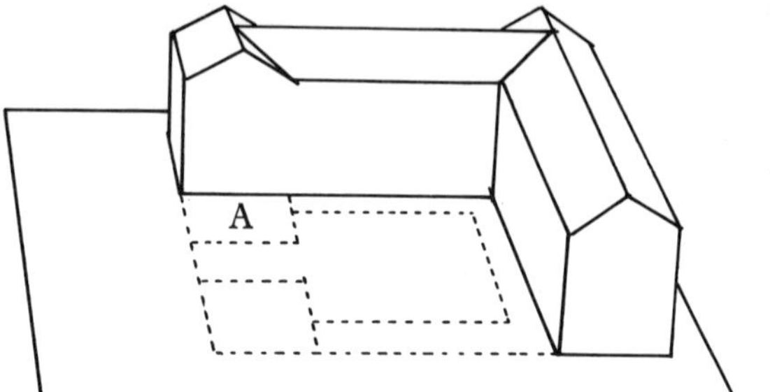

Glue the model to the base.

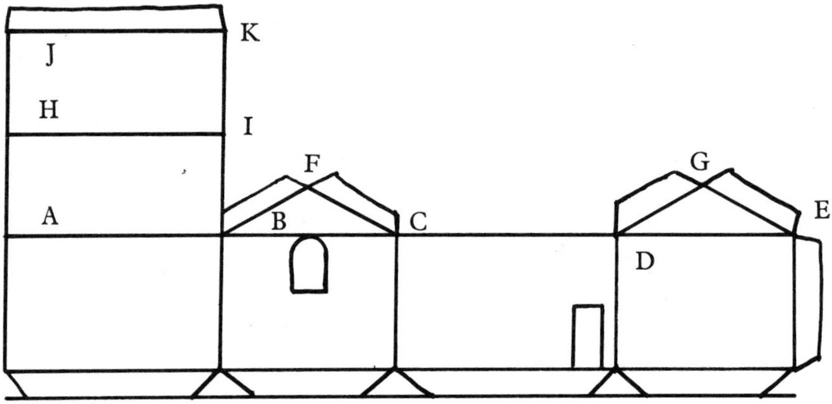

The bath house

Rule a base line 1cm ($\frac{1}{2}$in) above the lower edge of the card. Rule a 'wall height' line 45mm (1$\frac{3}{4}$in) above the base line. Measure along both lines AB 8cm (3$\frac{1}{4}$in), BC 6cm (2$\frac{1}{4}$in), CD 8cm (3$\frac{1}{4}$in) and DE 6cm (2$\frac{1}{4}$in).

Strike arcs of 3cm (1$\frac{1}{4}$in) from B, C, D and E. Points F and G will be where they cross. Continue lines up at A and B for roofs – 3cm (1$\frac{1}{4}$in) to AH and BI, and again 3cm (1$\frac{1}{4}$in) to HJ and IK. Add flaps and mark out the door and window. Cut out the model and glue it together. Place it in position on the base.

Entrance building

Mark this out in exactly the same way as for the bath house but with no door or window. Instead, draw a round-arched door in middle of the back wall, A, and a wide rectangular opening in the front, B. When you have cut, folded and glued everything together, cut out a piece of card the same size as B, but with flaps all round and a pair of doors, scored at dotted lines (diagram C),

A

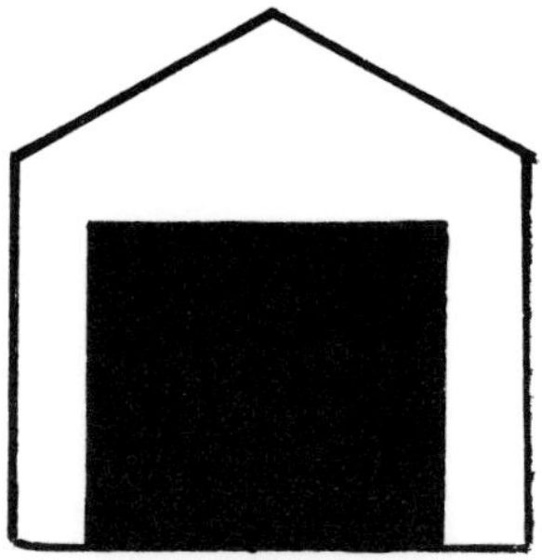
B

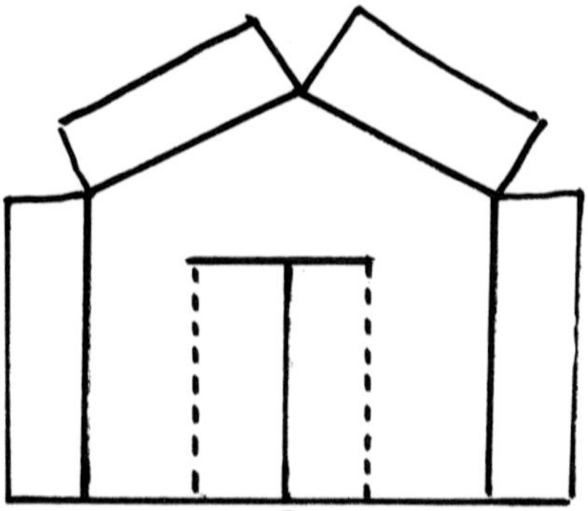

C

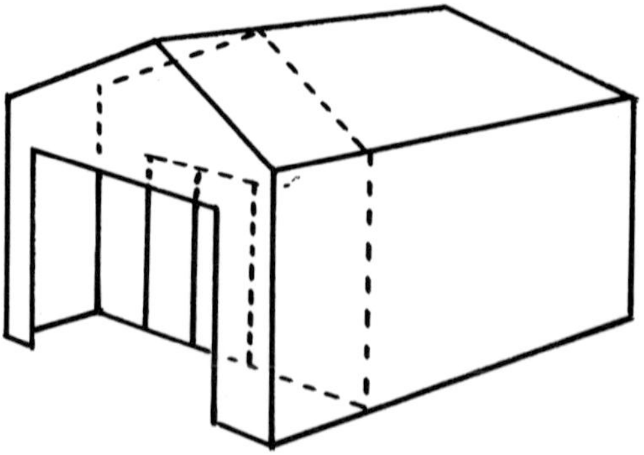

to open into the building. Glue this wall into position 1·25cm ($\frac{1}{2}$in) back from the entrance (diagram D).

Now build up a raised floor inside this front porch open area by cutting two lengths of balsa wood 6cm ($2\frac{1}{4}$in). Glue them to the base. Cut a piece of card $6 \times 1{\cdot}25$cm ($2\frac{1}{4} \times \frac{1}{2}$in) and glue it on top of the balsa. Next, glue strips of balsa all round the inside of entrance opening. Cut two lengths of drinking straw, or roll strips of paper to form pillars. Glue them into place.

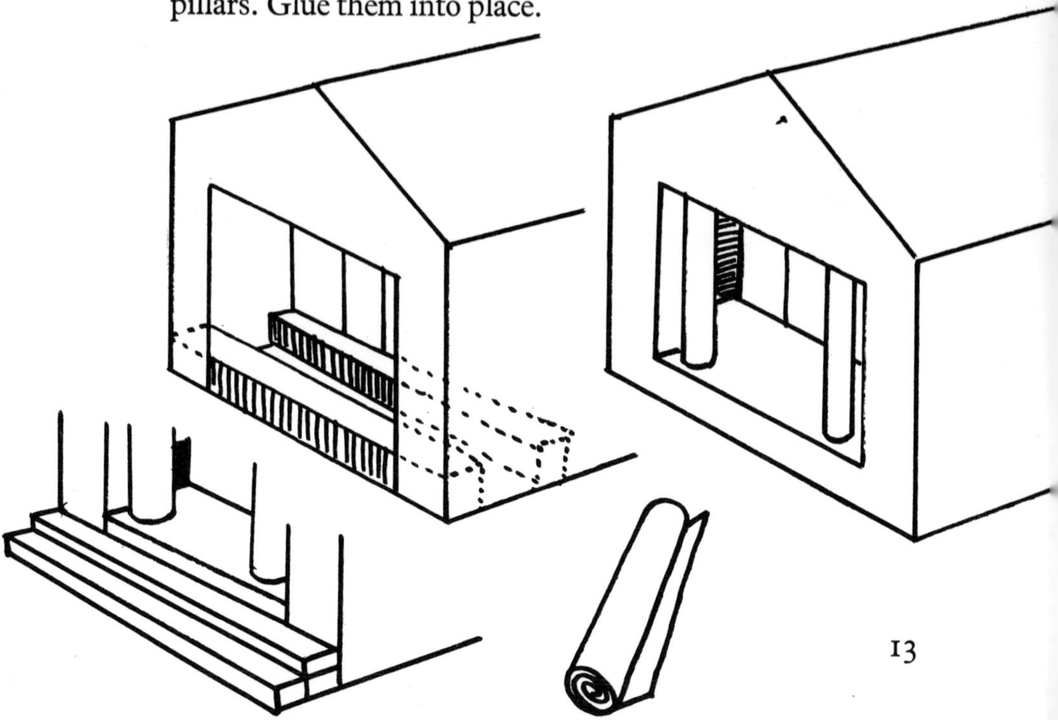

Add two steps. They could be flat strips of balsa, or built up with layers of card.

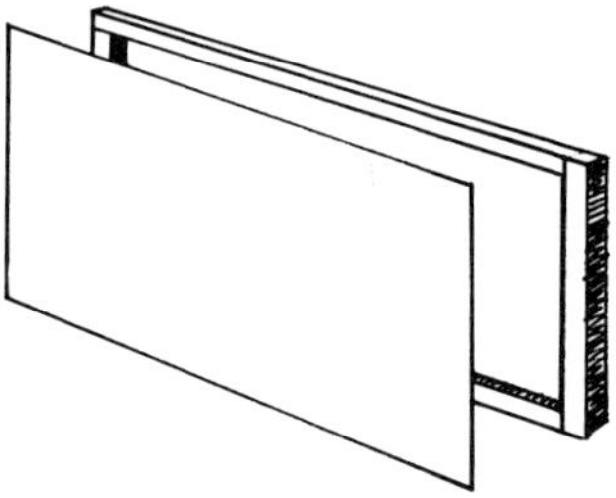

To complete the courtyard cut a length of card 4·5cm (1¾in) high and the exact width of the space between the bath house and the entrance buildings. Glue strips of balsa wood all round the edges between the two pieces of card to give the wall thickness. Make another wall for the remaining space.

Cloister

There is an open *cloister* round three sides of the yard. Mark it out on the base board 30mm (1¼in) wide. At the same time draw in paths and a circular pond. Leaving gaps where the paths lead into it, glue strips of balsa wood round the edge of the cloister (dotted lines on page 11). Cut twenty-four pillars out of drinking straws, 2cm (¾in) high, and glue them onto balsa wood 'wall'. Space them as on the plan. Cut three lengths of balsa wood to form a continuous top to the pillars.

Measure out the cloister roofs: Roof 1: AB 18cm (7in), AC 3·5cm (1½in), CD 15cm (5¾in)
Roof 2: EF 24cm (9½in), EG 3·5cm (1½in), GH and IJ 3cm (1¼in)

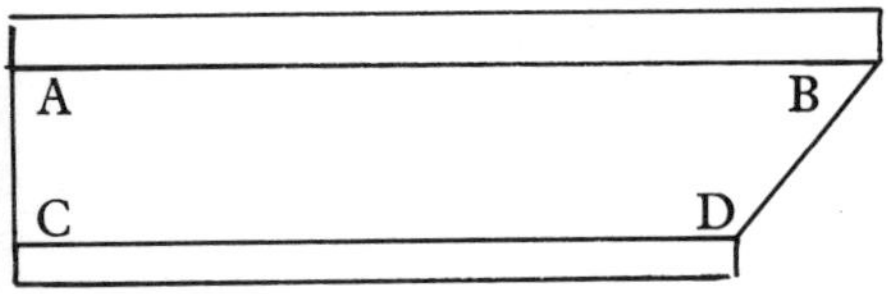

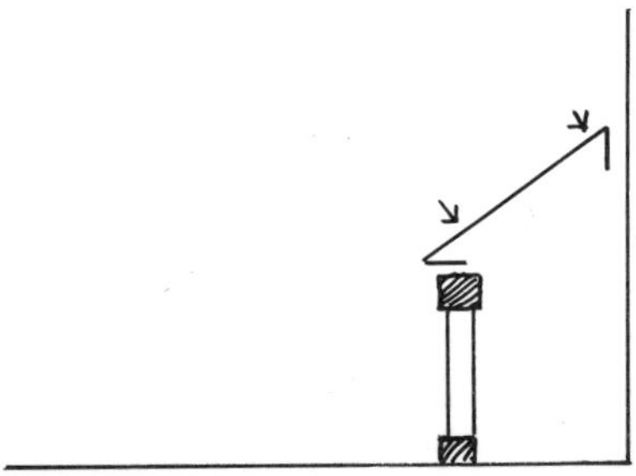

Roof 3: KL 18cm (7in), LN 3·5cm ($1\frac{1}{2}$in), MN 15cm ($5\frac{3}{4}$in)
Add flaps, cut out the roofs, fold and glue them in position.

Roofs
For all roofs, except the cloister, cut card to overlap by 3mm ($\frac{1}{8}$in) all round. Glue them on top.

Central pool
Cut two rings of card with an outer radius of 1·5cm ($\frac{1}{2}$in). Cut a circle of cellophane slightly smaller. Paint a circle of pale blue on the baseboard, then glue on the cellophane and lastly the two rings of card.

Hedges
For the clipped, low hedges lining the paths use strips of carpet underfelt, foam rubber or balsa wood. Cover them with baize or another soft green cloth that has a 'pile'.

Painting
Use both the colour chart on page 16 and the coloured drawing of the villa to help you paint your model of a Roman villa.

Colour mixing

It is usually best to wait until the model is complete and attached to the baseboard before starting to paint it. Use water colour – either liquid, powder colour, or from tubes. To obtain an even finish mix the paint to a creamy texture. A second coat may sometimes be needed.

Brick, stone, tiles, slates, wood and earth vary very much in colour according to their locality and age, but the chart opposite will give you a sound basis to work on.

You need only six colours:

white	yellow ochre	lemon yellow
vermilion	ultramarine	dark brown

Use the colour scale opposite to show you how much of each colour to use for:

A stone or gravel for roads and paths
B wood
C hedges and trees
D brick and tile
E grass
F slate (use more white for the colour of lead)

Texture

On the scale given in this book the surfaces of most buildings should be smooth and even but, if you wish to imitate rough stonework, flint, gravel paths, bare earth and other similar textures, there are two ways of doing it.

1 Mix sand or fine sawdust with the paint.

2 Apply a coat of paint in the normal way, but lighter or darker in tone than you eventually want. When the paint is dry, spray on a lighter or darker tone of the same colour using a simple fixative diffuser.

A

B

C

D

E

F

Norman keep

After their invasion of Britain in 1066, the Normans built strong, stone castles all over the country to protect themselves. Many of these, like the Tower of London, are still almost the same as they were when they were built. There was usually a massive, square keep, containing a great hall, barrack rooms and store rooms. The keep stood in the middle of an irregular-shaped bailey, or courtyard, which had a high wall round it, with battlements and a fortified gatehouse.

This model is based on the castles at Rochester, Dover, Hedingham and Newcastle.

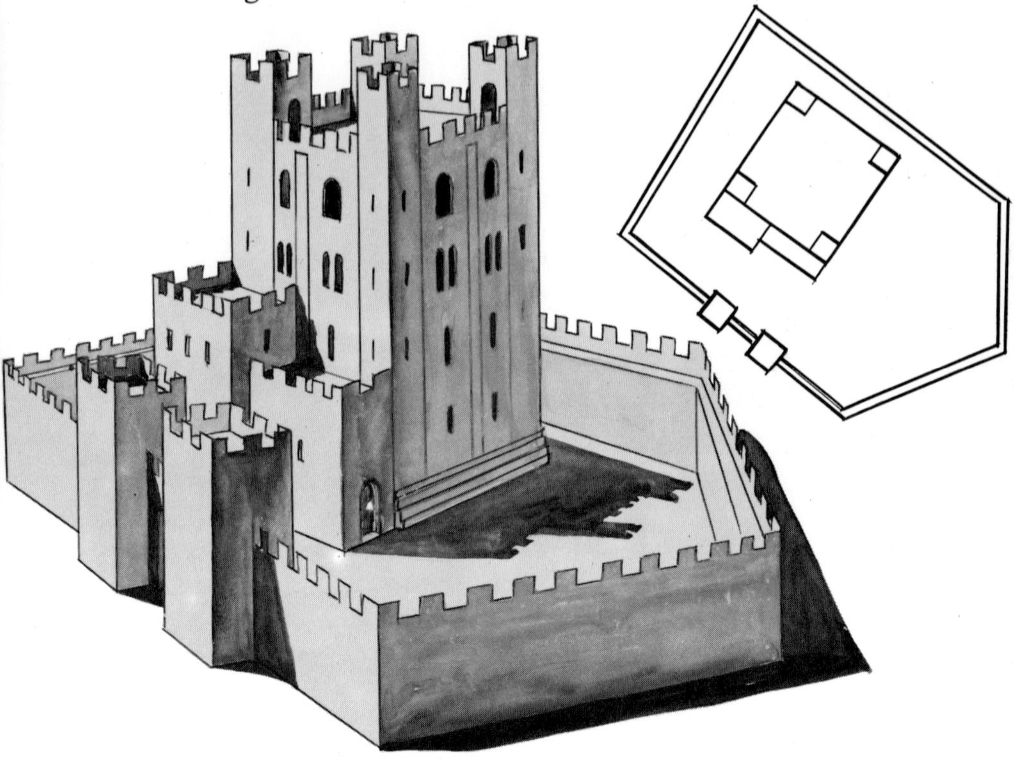

Opposite: Shakespeare's birthplace – the model and the real thing

Rule base line A across card 1·5cm ($\frac{3}{4}$in) above the edge of the card. Rule line B for the top of the main building 20cm (8in) above the base line. Rule line C 1cm ($\frac{1}{2}$in) above that for battlements. Mark out four equal sides 15cm (6in) wide. Add side flap X and mark out flaps below the base line. Mark out an equal space of 2·5cm (1in) on each side of the corner lines positioning the corner towers.

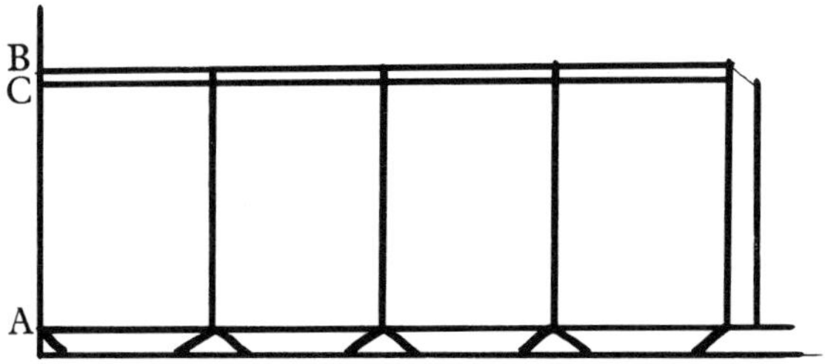

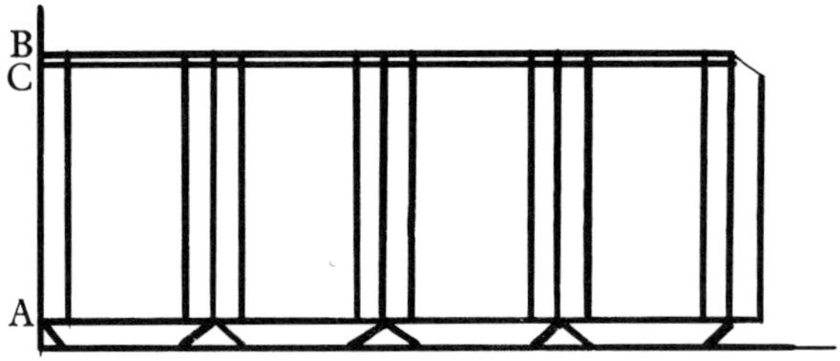

Mark out *battlements* and windows on each of the four sides. The drawing shows one complete side. Draw a pencil line down the middle to make sure the windows are evenly placed. Make sure they are at the same height across all four sides.

Cut out all round with scissors. Use a knife for cutting out battlements and windows.

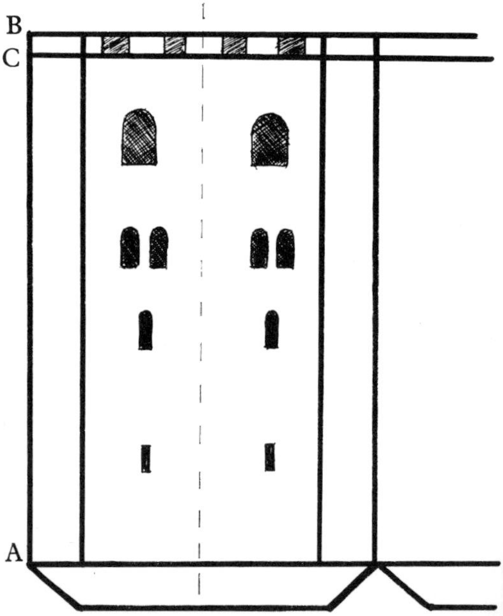

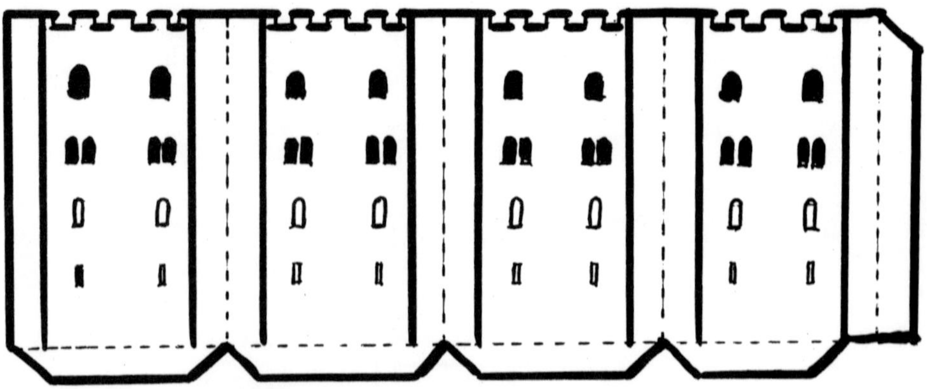

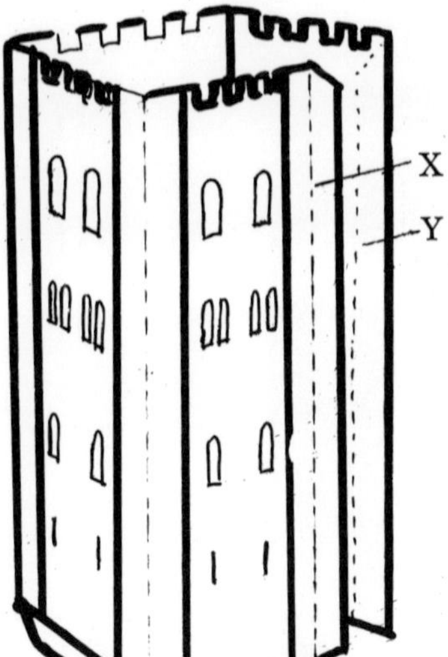

Score all the corners and flaps (dotted lines in diagram). Fold the tower into shape and glue the vertical flap X to the inside edge of the tower, Y.

For the flat roof mark out a square 1mm ($1\frac{1}{10}$in) shorter than 15 × 15cm (6 × 6in). Add flaps to each side deep enough to reach below the top storey windows. Before gluing the roof into position, trace the outline of the windows onto the flaps. Mark out inner window frames, slightly smaller than those in outer wall. Cut out the windows and glue roof in place.

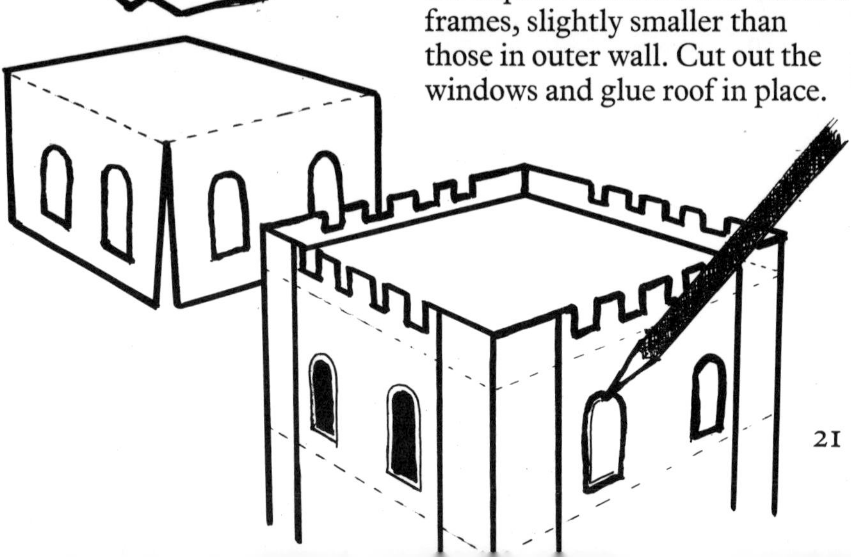

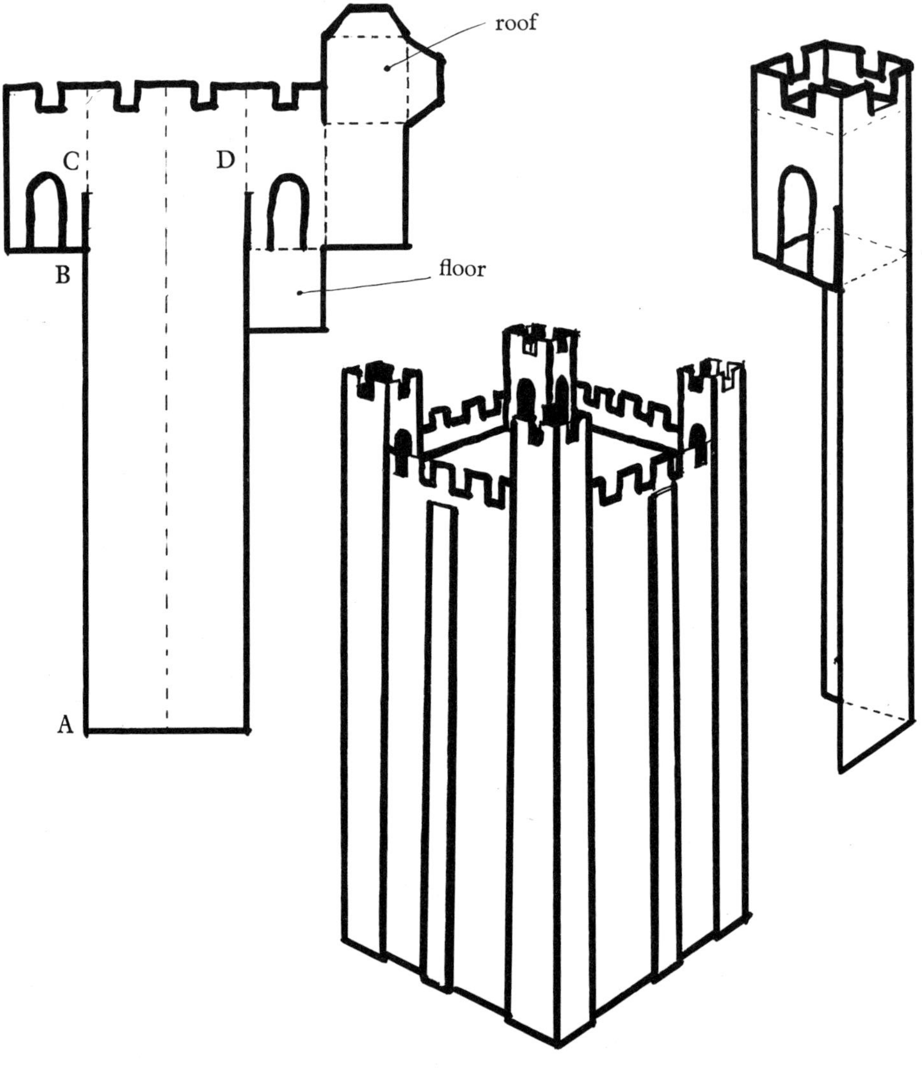

Mark out four corner towers 23cm (9in) high. Each must have four sides and a flap 2·5cm (1in) wide. Be sure that height AB is the same as height of the flat roof of the main building, and that slots at C and D are the same height as the top of battlements. Cut out the towers and score and fold all dotted lines. Glue together each tower before attaching it to the main model. Cut out narrow strips of cardboard and glue them down the centre of each wall for *buttresses*.

The fore-buildings

Fore-buildings protected the entrance to the keep, which was usually on the first floor level and reached by an outside staircase.

The dotted lines show their position against side wall of the keep. Mark out both buildings, cut them out, fold on dotted lines and glue them together.

To give the effect of thickness to the arched doorway, glue a piece of card behind the opening and cut out a smaller arch. Repeat this and, finally, glue a plain piece of card behind the entrance to make the door.

B

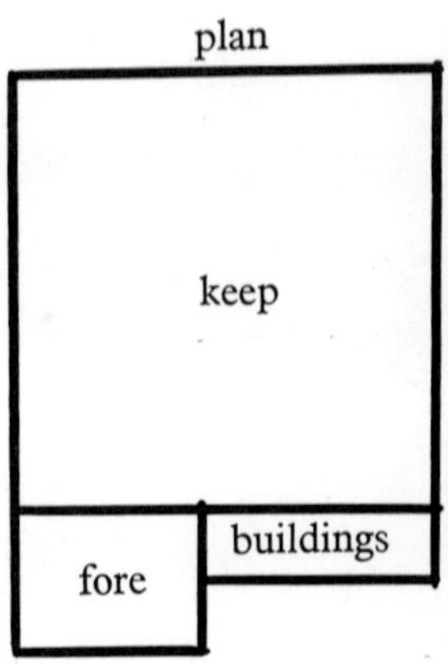

A

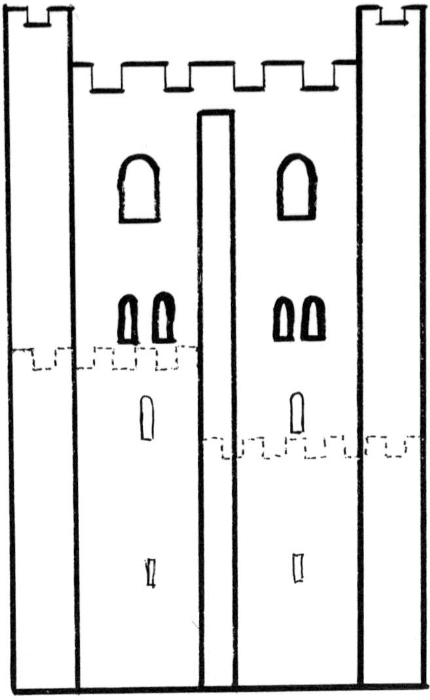

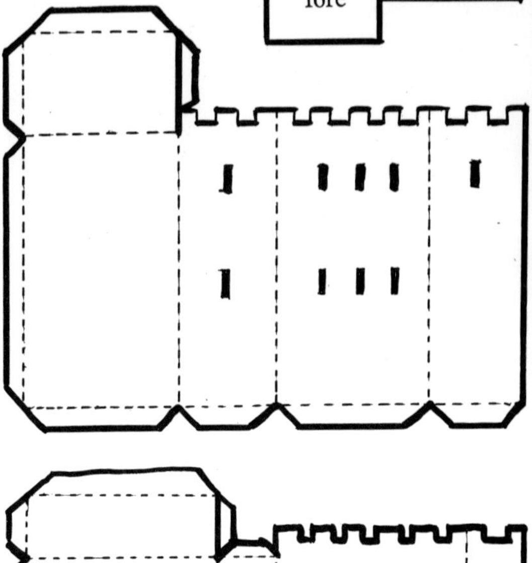

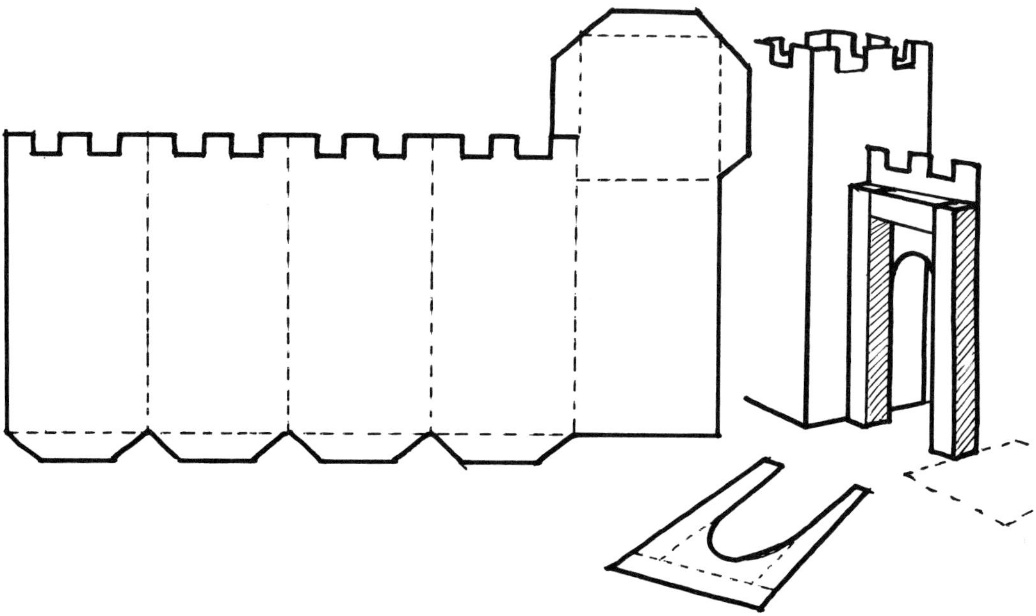

The keep and fore-buildings can now be glued to each other and to the centre of the baseboard.

Gatehouse and curtain walls

Cut out two square-planned towers 10cm (4in) high. The four walls and also the flap should be 5cm (2in) wide. For the gateway, cut out two semi-circular archways 3cm (1½in) wide. One should have battlements and the other should be shorter with a flat top. Glue lengths of balsa along the top and down the sides of the archway so they are sandwiched between the two pieces of card.

Glue the parts of the gatehouse to a baseboard following the ground plan in page 19. Cut out the outer, battlemented, face of the walls 8cm (3in) high. Make a double width 'crenel' (the raised, solid part of the battlement) at all the corners. Glue lengths of balsa wood along the base edge at 1cm (½in) below the battlements. Glue the walls onto baseboard, starting next to the gatehouse towers.

Measure and cut strips of card for the inner face of the walls. They should be as high as the top of the strips of balsa. Glue them in place.

Painting

Walls and roofs – light stone
Doors – plain wood
Ground – grass, with rough earth paths leading through the entrance gates to the door in the fore-building. Use the colour mixing chart on pages 16–17 to help you.

Extras

'Lean-to' buildings were often built round the inside of the curtain walls. They might be stables, barns and huts for the peasants and sometimes even a small church. Make these in the same way as the cloisters for the Roman villa (see page 14).

Medieval manor house

This model is closely based on Great Chalfield, Wiltshire, which was built in about 1450. The builder retained the Great Hall, 'screens' and *solar* of earlier manors. He also increased the number of living rooms and was one of the first to achieve a nearly symmetrical design for the north, or entrance, front. This idea which became very usual in Tudor times.

The photograph is taken looking at the back, or south side, of the house.

This is a plan of the manor house, looking from above. It shows the roofs, chimneys, buttresses and *oriel* windows (bay windows built out from the wall).

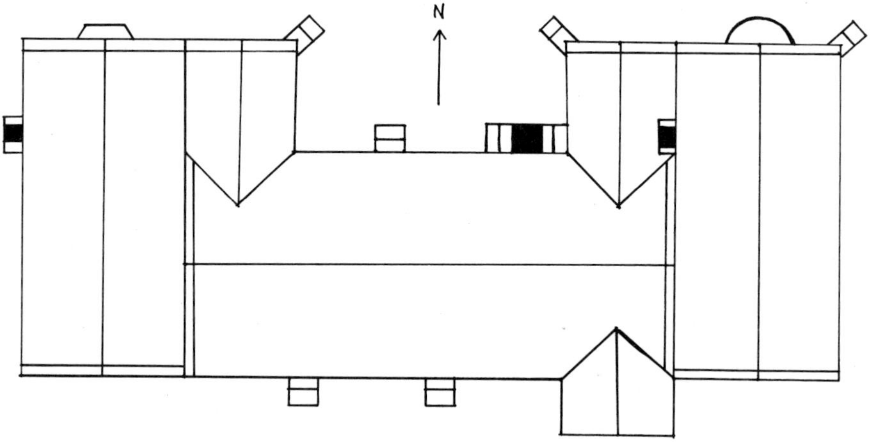

The suggested size for the model is 30cm (12in) long, 12cm ($4\frac{3}{4}$in) wide, and 10cm (4in) high.

The Great Hall (central building) and two wings should be made separately.

The Great Hall

Rule a base line 1cm ($\frac{1}{2}$in) above the lower edge of the card. Rule a wall height line A 6cm ($2\frac{1}{2}$in) above the base line.

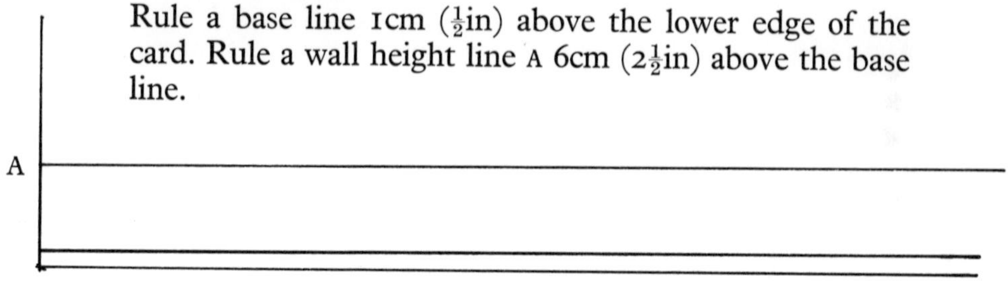

Starting from the left on both lines, measure AB 8cm ($3\frac{1}{4}$in), BC 18cm (7in), CD 8cm ($3\frac{1}{4}$in), DE 18cm (7in).

Add gable ends F and G by using compasses to strike arcs of 6cm ($2\frac{1}{2}$in) from A, B, C and D.

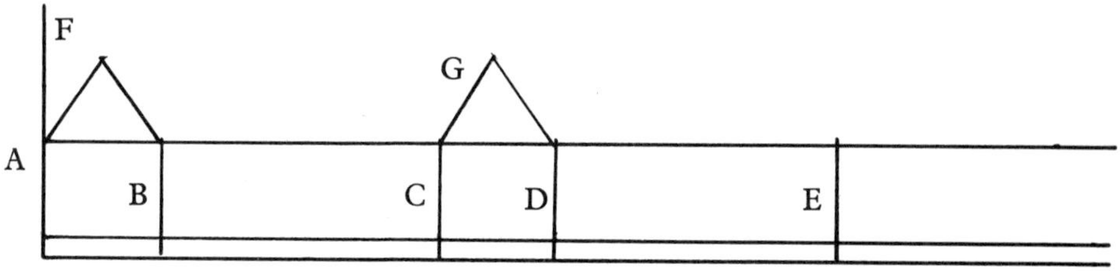

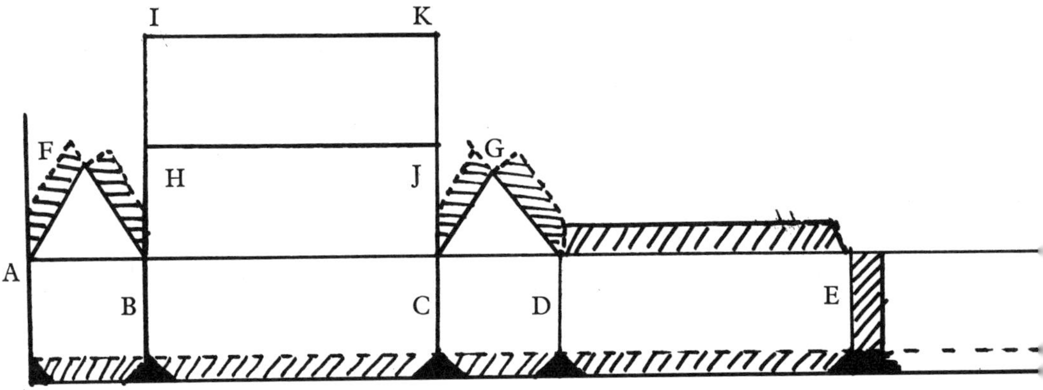

Continue lines up at B and C for roof. BH, HI, CJ and JK should all measure 6cm (2½in). Add flaps (shaded in diagram).

Before cutting out the main hall, mark out on the long walls the position of the entrance hall and other projecting buildings. Each should be 4cm (1½in) wide.
Mark out the windows, with lower edges 2·5cm (1in) from the ground. Rule a second line 2·5cm (1in) above this for the base of the arches. Measure window spacings: FG 3cm (1¼in), GH 2cm (¾in), HI 2·5cm (1in), IJ 2cm (¾in).

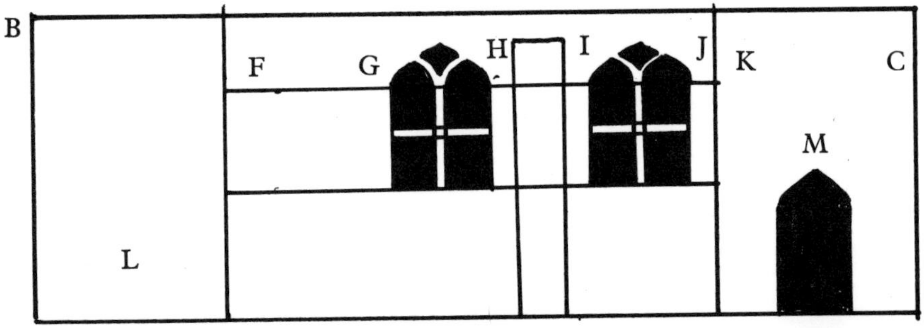

On the other long wall mark out LM 2cm ($\frac{3}{4}$in), MN 2cm ($\frac{3}{4}$in), NO 2·5cm (1in), OP 2cm ($\frac{3}{4}$in), PQ 2·5cm (1in), QR 2cm (1in).

Mark out all the windows as shown in the diagrams. Use a knife to cut out all the areas shaded black. Back the windows with clear cellophane.

Score all corners, flaps and roof edges of the main building. Fold and glue.

East wing

Draw the base line and top of the wall line in the same way as for the Great Hall.

Begin measuring at the left with a flap 1cm ($\frac{1}{2}$in) wide, then AB 6cm ($2\frac{1}{2}$in), BC 12cm ($4\frac{1}{2}$in), CD 6cm ($2\frac{1}{2}$in), DE 4cm ($1\frac{1}{2}$in), EF 4cm ($1\frac{1}{2}$in). Add a flap 1cm ($\frac{1}{2}$in) wide.

Add *gable*-ends ABG and CDH by striking an arc of 5cm (2in) from A, B, C and D. Continue the vertical lines at B and C to make the roof. Mark out BI, CJ, IK and KL 5cm (2in). Add smaller gable-end DEM by striking arcs 3cm ($1\frac{1}{4}$in) from D and E. Continue vertical lines at E and F for roofs. Mark out EN, NP, FO and OQ 3cm ($1\frac{1}{4}$in). Continue NO for 2cm ($\frac{3}{4}$in) to R. Join FR and QR. Add flaps.

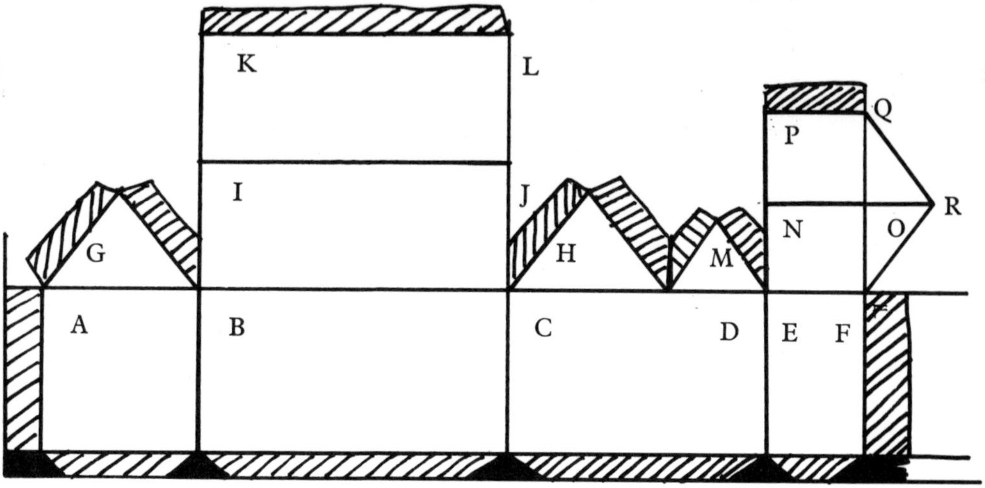

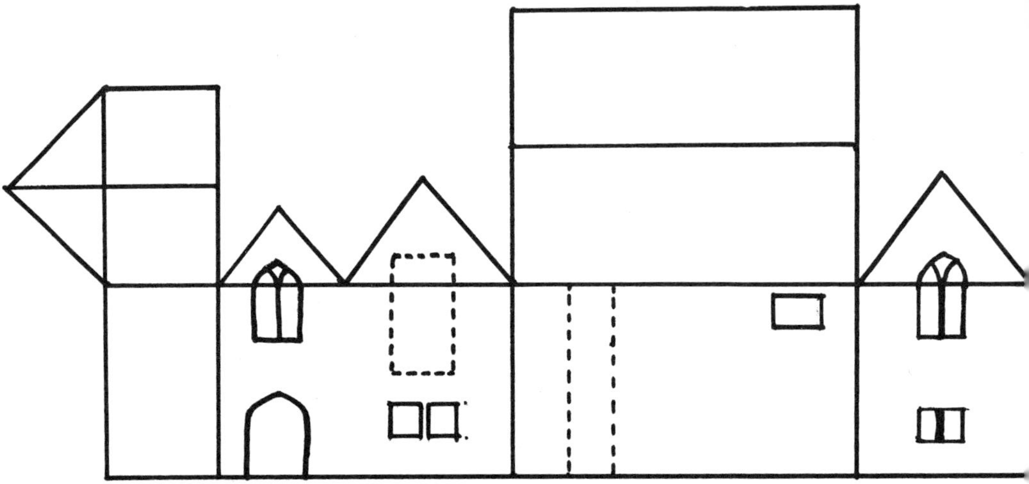

right (or west) wing

Mark out the position of the windows and that of the oriel window shown by the dotted line – 2×3·5cm ($\frac{3}{4}$×1$\frac{1}{2}$in). Keep the oriel and gable windows central.

West wing
Mark out the right, or west wing exactly the same as the east wing – but in reverse. Use the same measurements, but work from the right edge of the cardboard. Mark out the windows, door and space for chimney.

Cut out both wings and glue cellophane onto the backs of the windows. Score, fold and glue both wings. Glue them to the central Great Hall.

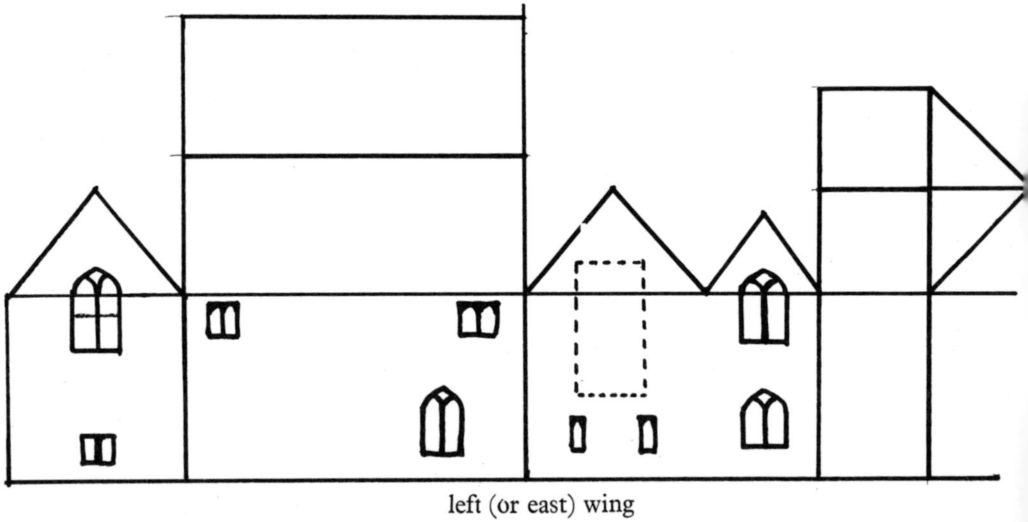

left (or east) wing

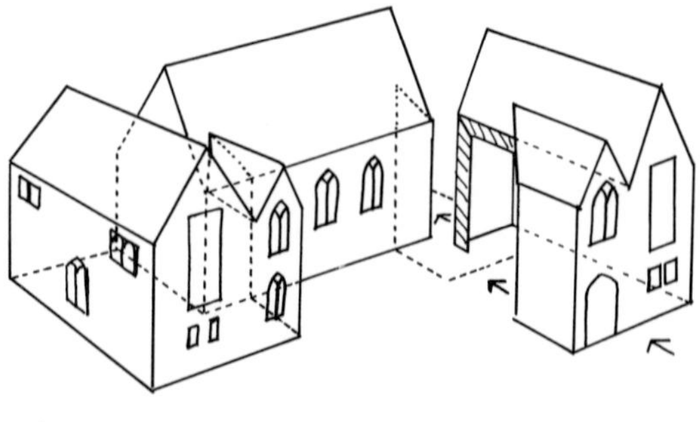

East oriel window

Make this in thick drawing paper.

Begin by marking out the rectangle ABCD, $2 \times 3{\cdot}5$cm ($\frac{3}{4} \times 1\frac{1}{2}$in). This is the back, which will be glued to the gable of the East wing. The floor and roof are not complete semi-circles. Draw a centre line and mark E and F 2mm ($\frac{1}{8}$in) inside to make centres for curves between A and B, C and D.

Measure BH and CG 3cm ($1\frac{1}{8}$in) for the curved front of the window. Divide it into six equal vertical spaces. Now draw in the windows. Add the band of ornament above the line BH. Add flaps to roof and floor and flap GHIJ – the same size as ABCD. This should be painted black on the reverse side to be seen through the window. Cut out the windows and back them with cellophane. Cut fold and glue it together.

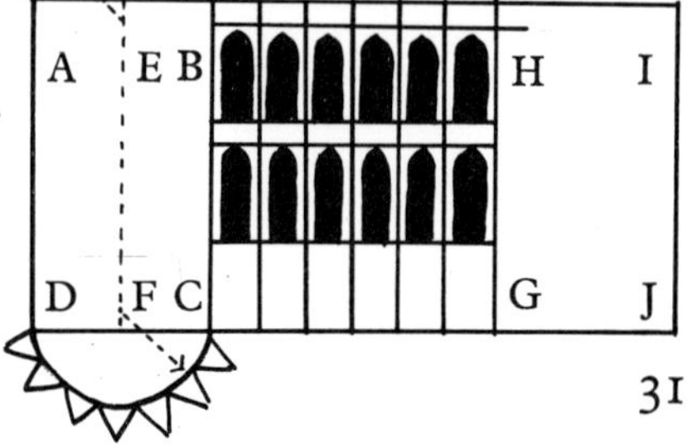

Before gluing it to the building, turn the oriel upside down and add four or five thicknesses of card of smaller and smaller size to obtain the bowl-like effect of the underside of the window. Glue a strip of balsa to the wall to 'support' the whole window and attach thin strips of balsa or card between each window, and narrow strips of card horizontally for mouldings at K and L (see previous page).

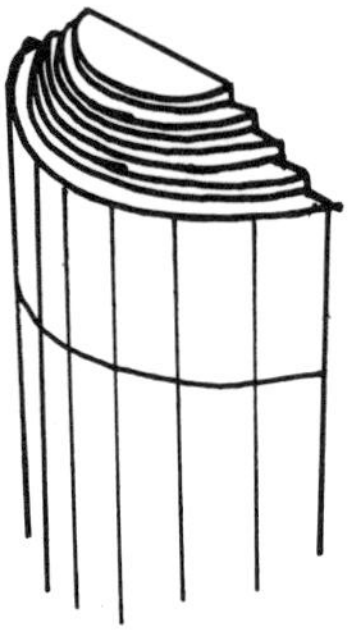

West oriel window

Mark out the back ABCD 3·5 × 3cm ($1\frac{1}{2} \times 1\frac{1}{4}$in). Mark out the floor with DE and FC 1cm ($\frac{1}{2}$in) and EF 2cm ($\frac{3}{4}$in).

The diagram shows how to do this. Mark out the three sides of the oriel BG 1cm ($\frac{1}{2}$in), GH 2cm ($\frac{3}{4}$in), HI 1cm ($\frac{1}{2}$in). Mark out horizontal lines and windows as in the diagram. For the roof, strike arcs of 3cm (1in) from G and H, measure GJ and HK 1·5cm ($\frac{1}{2}$in). Find L and

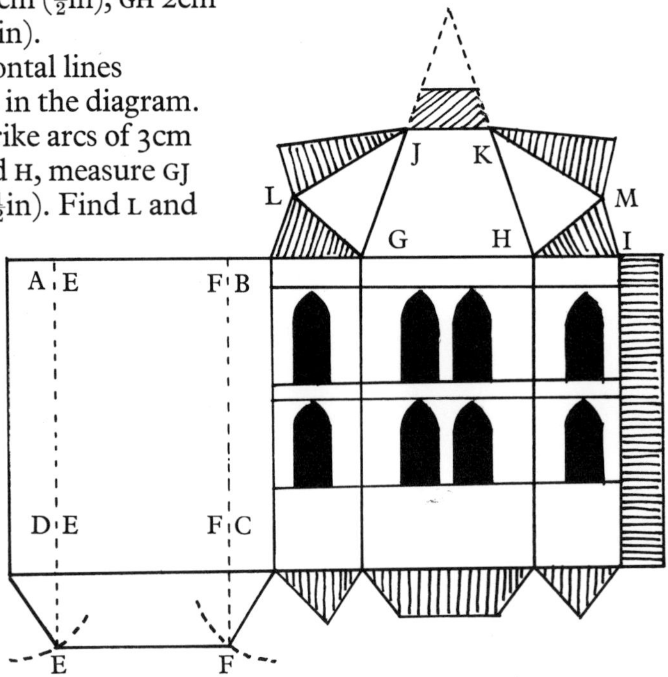

M by striking arcs of 1·5cm ($\frac{1}{2}$in) from J and K, and arcs of 1cm ($\frac{1}{2}$in) from G and H. Join up GLJ and HKM to make the sides of the roof. Add flaps, cut out and fold. Glue cellophane behind windows and paint the back wall black.

In assembling, glue one flap at a time and allow it to dry before gluing the next one.

North front

Add the chimney of the Great Hall and four buttresses. Use lengths of balsa wood 1 × 0·5 cm ($\frac{1}{2}$ × $\frac{1}{4}$in) thickness. Cut two lengths 12cm (5in) for the centre section. Add two lengths 7cm (3in). Cut the tops to slope. Add two more lengths 2cm ($\frac{3}{4}$in). Glue all the lengths together and fix in place (see plan).

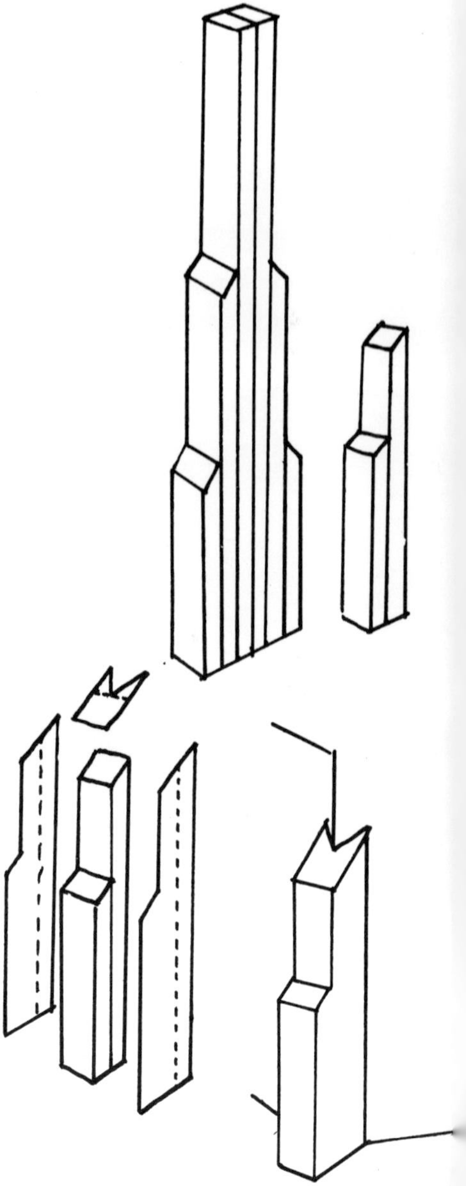

Make the buttresses between the Great Hall windows next. The tallest piece should end just below roof level; the shorter piece just above lower edge of windows.

Begin the three corner buttresses in the same way and with the same measurements as the others. Then trace round the complete buttress onto card, adding 5mm ($\frac{1}{4}$in) width on the tall side. Cut out six of these pieces of card and glue them on to the balsa. Now glue the completed buttresses to the corners at an angle (see plan). Cut card roofs to fit.

When first built the south side of Great Chalfield faced into a square courtyard, surrounded by store rooms.

South wing

Measure out AB 2cm (¾in), BC 4cm (1½in), CD 2cm (¾in), BE 6cm (2½in), EH, EG, FG and HI 3cm (1¼in). Find J by striking arcs of 3·5cm (1¼in) from K and L. The sloping roofs may have to be altered slightly to fit when you are ready to attach the wing to the main building. Mark out flaps, door and window. Cut out and glue together.

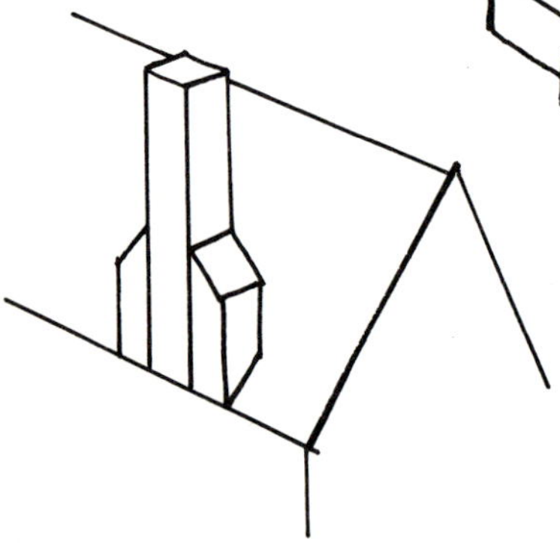

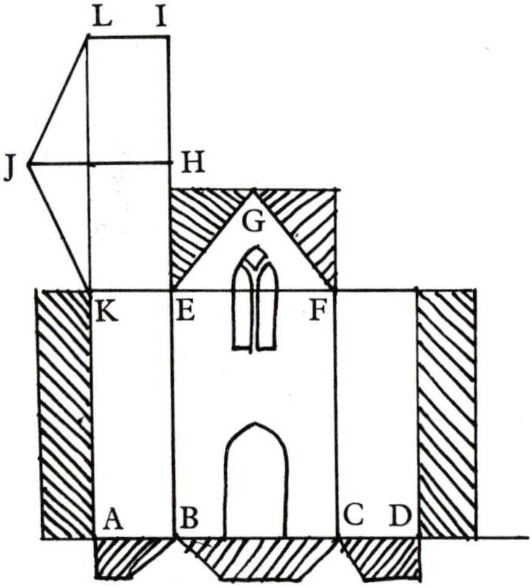

Chimneys

The chimney on the west wall should be the same height as the Great Hall chimney – 12cm (5in) – but only needs one step on each side of 7cm (3in). The third chimney is much shorter 3·5cm (1½in) in the centre and with very short steps. Glue the three pieces together and allow to dry before cutting the base to fit the slope of the roof.

Roofs

Build up all gable-ends by 0·5cm (¼in) with lengths of balsa wood or several thicknesses of cardboard 0·5cm (¼in) wide.

Take great care to make joints as neat as possible, and glue in position so that the end of gable stays flat.

When you have built up all the gable-ends, fit in a second thickness of roof to overlap all the walls by 0·25cm ($\frac{1}{8}$in). Cut them carefully to fit round the chimneys.

Finally, cut thin strips of paper and fold them down the middle before gluing on as ridge tiles.

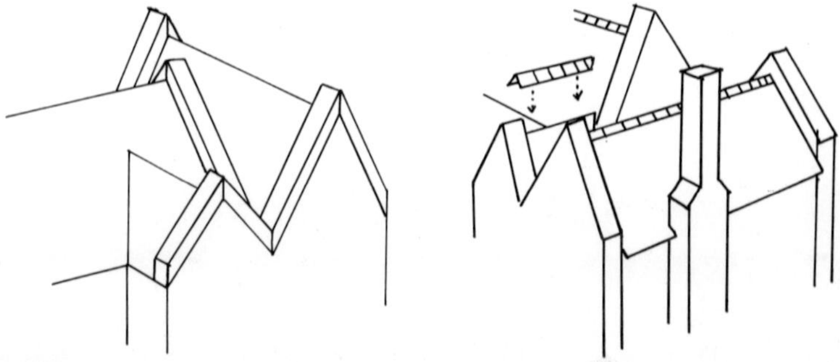

Dripstones

Every window and door in the building was protected from the rain by a dripstone, or hoodmould – a thin, projecting ledge of stone which followed exactly the shape of the top of the door or window.

Leave a gap of 2mm ($\frac{1}{10}$in) between the dripstone and top of each window or door. Cut away the inside of the shape first, and decorate the ends with a tiny bead or piece of balsa.

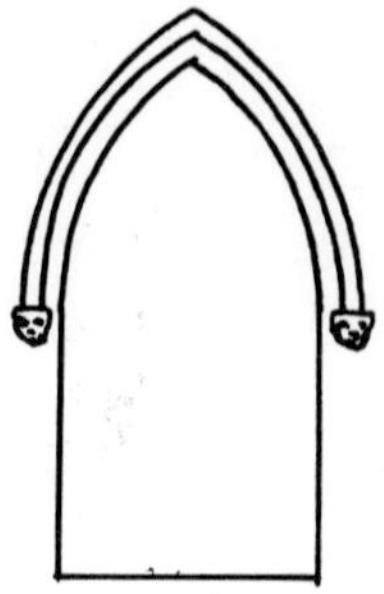

Painting

All the walls are of stone, but the window and door frames, dripstones, buttresses, chimneys and the roofs of gables are of smoother limestone. Paint these a shade or two lighter than the main walls (see colour photograph on page 35). The roofs are slightly darker than the walls and faintly mottled with an ochre-coloured lichen. Follow the colour chart on pages 16 and 17 if you need help in mixing your colours.

Opposite: Two views of the White House, showing the square front entrance and curved back

Shakespeare's birthplace

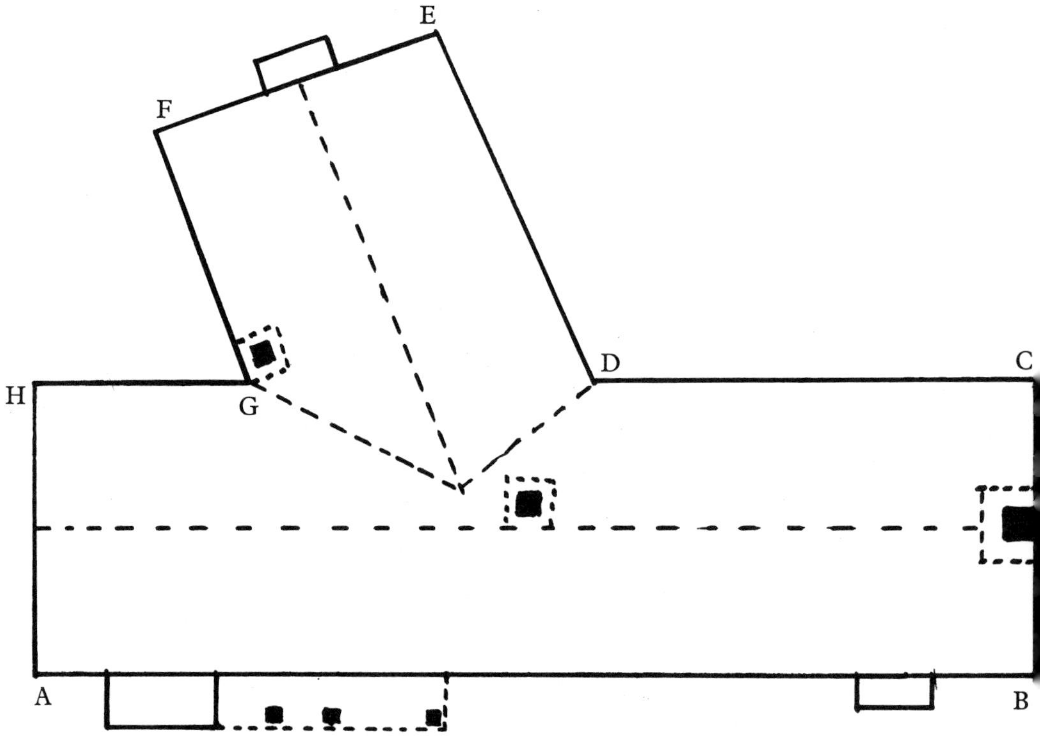

Apart from its interest as Shakespeare's birthplace, this house in Stratford-on-Avon, Warwickshire, is typical of timber-framed buildings all over England, in town and country. Though most of them date from the Tudor period, many are very much older. In Shakespeare's time, part of the ground floor was used as a shop.

There is no attempt at symmetry in the planning of rooms or windows, and the wing at the back sticks out at a very odd angle as is shown by the ground plan below. The whole of the house, including the awkwardly-shaped back wing, can be made in one piece, making the model stronger and easier to assemble – only the roofs, oriel windows, chimneys and porch will need to be made separately.

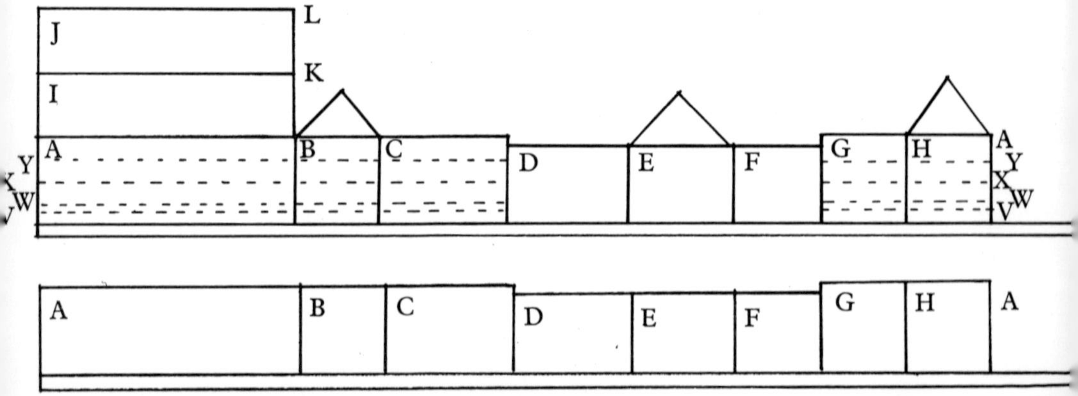

Starting at the lower, long edge of a sheet of card, mark off a base-line 1cm ($\frac{1}{2}$in) above the lower edge. Measure the height of the main building walls: AA 6·25cm ($2\frac{1}{2}$in).
Mark off AB 20cm (8in), BC 5·75cm ($2\frac{1}{4}$in), CD 9cm ($3\frac{1}{2}$in). The back wing is 1·25cm ($\frac{1}{2}$in) lower than main building, so DE should be 7·5cm (3in), EF 6·25cm ($2\frac{1}{2}$in), FG 5cm (2in).

Now return to original height of walls which is 6·25cm ($2\frac{1}{2}$in). Make GH 4·5cm ($1\frac{3}{4}$in), HA 5·75cm ($2\frac{1}{4}$in).

Mark out triangular gable-ends at BC, EF and HA by striking arcs of 4·5cm ($\frac{3}{4}$in). Continue verticals at A and B for roofs: AI, IK, BK and KL should all be 4·5cm ($1\frac{3}{4}$in).

Windows, doors and timbering
Before taking each side in detail, rule these lines which are the same all the way round the house: V-V, the low stone wall on which the timber frame rests 7·5mm ($\frac{1}{4}$in) above the base line. Just above this, rule a line W-W to represent the thickness of the lowest horizontal beam. Above this line, the layout of timbers and windows in the back wing is different to the main building, so rule the following lines only on sides AB, BC, CD, GH, HA. X-X supports the floor of the upper storey and divides the building

almost in half. It is 2·5cm (1in) above W-W. Y-Y divides the upper storey in half and supports the windows, 1·5cm ($\frac{1}{2}$in) above W-W.

At first, draw all the timbers with a single pencil line. Later, when you paint them, make X-X twice as thick as the others. The diagonal and short timbers are slightly narrower than the others.

The street front

This is side AB. Begin by marking the position of the three 'dormer' windows along the top line: 6cm (2$\frac{1}{4}$in), 2·25cm (1in), 3cm (1$\frac{1}{4}$in), 2·25cm (1in), 1·25cm ($\frac{1}{2}$in), 5·25cm (2in). Repeat these measurements along the base line and join them up. Then continue the first four lines up for another 1·5cm ($\frac{3}{4}$in) for the two small dormers. Strike arcs of 1·5cm ($\frac{3}{4}$in) for the gable-ends. For the wide gable at extreme right, strike arcs of 4cm (1$\frac{1}{2}$in).

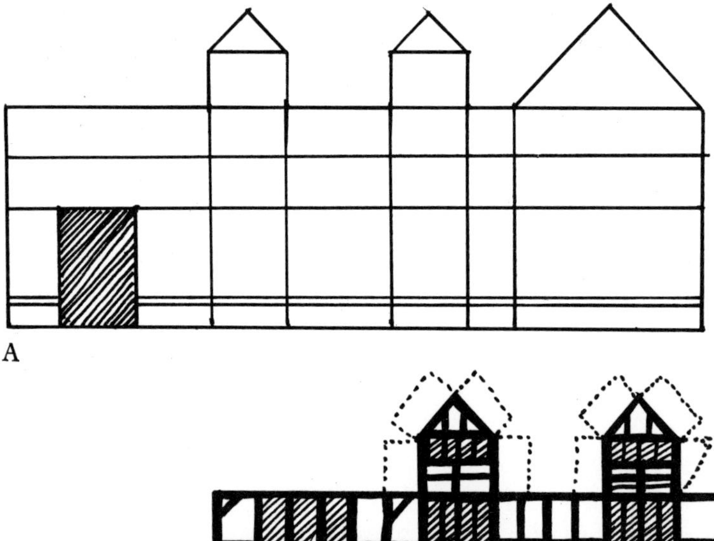

A

On the ground floor, mark out the position of the projecting window – 1·5cm (½in) from A, and 2·25cm (1in) wide.

With these main lines drawn in, it should be easy to mark out all remaining timbers, windows, doors, etc, using the diagram as a guide. Add flaps, which are shown as dotted lines in the diagram.

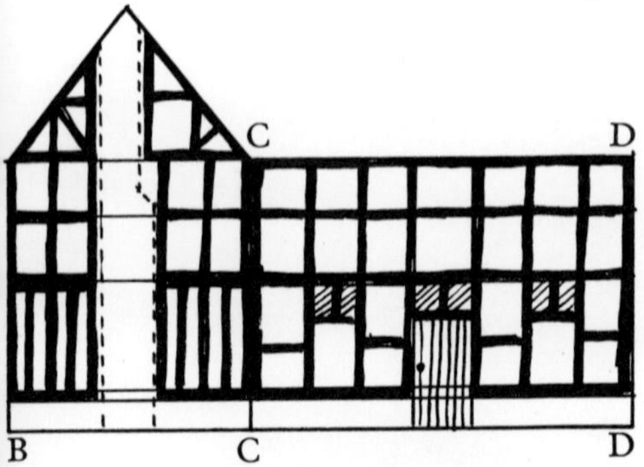

Side and back

These are sides BC and CD. The dotted line in the diagram shows the position of the chimney in the centre of BC. Place a door in the centre of CD. Mark out the timbers as before.

The back wing

This is made up of sides DE, EF and FC. Draw a horizontal line across all three sides at a height of 2·5cm (1in). Mark off the following points along both roof and base lines of DE: 1·25cm (½in), 1·25cm (½in), 1·75cm (¾in), 1·75cm (¾in), 1·5cm (½in).

Raise window heights 5mm (¼in), add gable-ends and flaps. Divide the top half of EF into six vertically. The oriel window uses two centre sections. The door is to the right of centre.

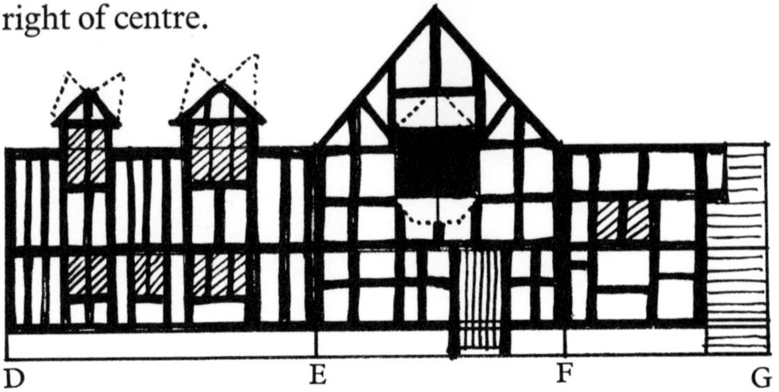

FG is very irregular and is partly taken up by a stone chimney let into the wall (shaded in diagram).

These two photographs of the back of the house show the back wing and its angle to the house. In the bottom photograph one of the gable windows is visible to the left of the tree. In the other photograph you can just see the oriel window and door on the end of the wing and the top of the stone chimney.

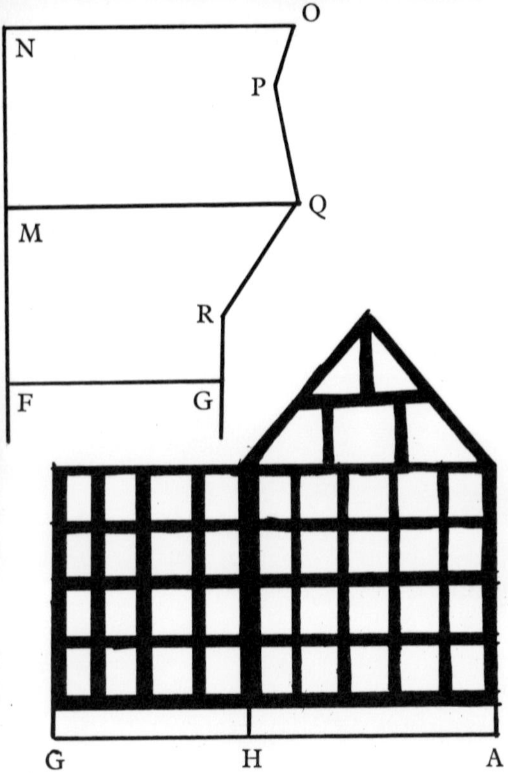

Back and final side

These sides – GH and HA – are very plain with no windows or doors.

Back wing roof

Now, mark out the roof of the back wing above the wall FG. Continue the vertical line from F 4·5cm ($1\frac{3}{4}$in) to M, and again 4·5cm ($1\frac{3}{4}$in) to N. Measure NO 7·5cm (3in), MQ 7·5cm (3in). To find P, strike arcs of 1·5cm ($\frac{1}{2}$in) from O, and 3cm ($1\frac{1}{2}$in) from Q. From G continue vertical 1·5cm ($\frac{1}{2}$in) to R, and join RQ.

Assembling

Add flaps (black in diagram). Cut out all round. Cut out windows and glue cellophane to back them. Cut carefully with a knife round the flaps of the dormer windows on the front AB. Remember, when folding the roof back, not to fold the dormers too. Score and fold all corners, roofs and flaps. Glue the whole building together, making sure that each flap is firmly glued before gluing the next one. When complete, glue the building to the baseboard.

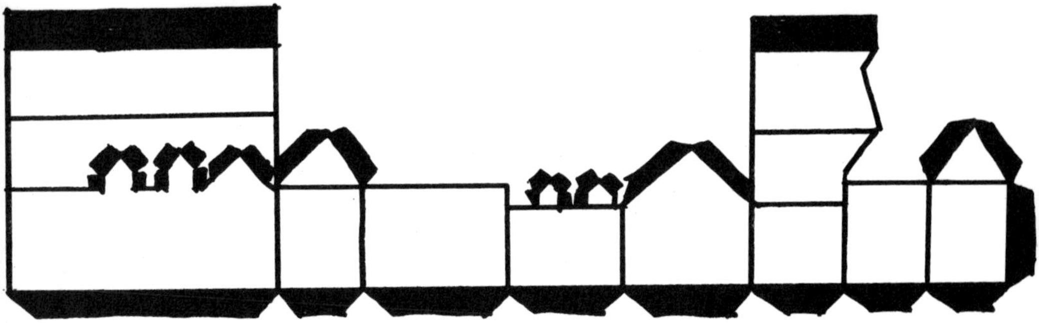

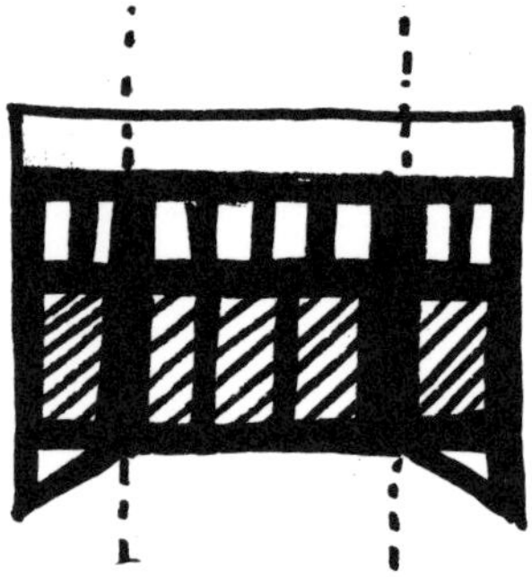

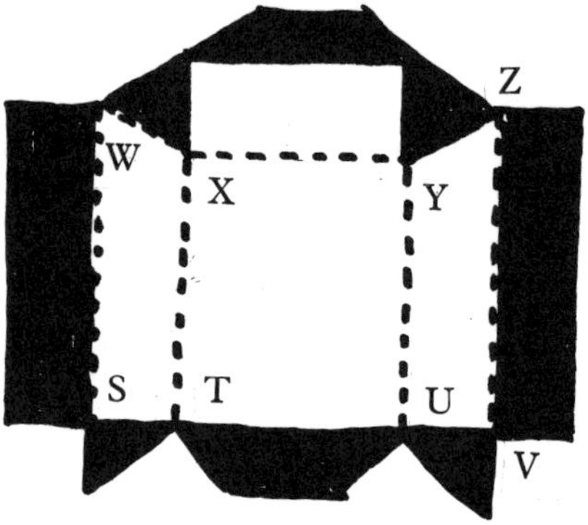

Front porch

To complete the front of building, first make the ground floor projecting window. Draw ST 1cm ($\frac{1}{2}$in), TU 2·5cm (1in), UV 1cm ($\frac{1}{2}$in). Heights: SW and VZ 3·5cm (1 $\frac{3}{10}$in), TX and UY 3cm (1$\frac{1}{5}$in). Use compasses to find the width of the roof, which should be the same as XW and VZ. Add flaps (black in diagram).

Mark out timbering and windows. Cut out windows, back with cellophane and glue to main building.

Cut three lengths of square-sectioned balsa wood 2mm ($\frac{1}{10}$in) thick for vertical posts 2·5cm (1in) high, and one length 7cm (2$\frac{3}{4}$in) for the horizontal '*lintel*'. Glue them in position (see diagram). Cut out a rectangular piece of card for the roof of the porch, overlapping slightly all round. Glue it to the roof of the projecting window and lintel.

For the gable over the front door, cut a triangle of card, with AB 1·5cm ($\frac{3}{4}$in). Fold along AB. Carefully cut pieces of balsa to fit under the roof slope, and glue it in position.

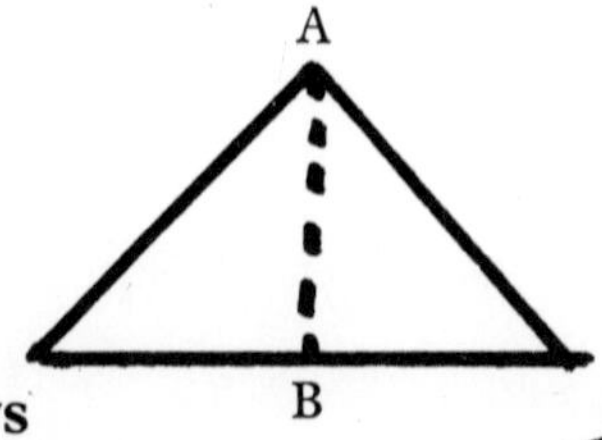

Oriel windows

One is for the front of the building (see page 18) and the other for the end of the back wing (see page 43). Both are identical

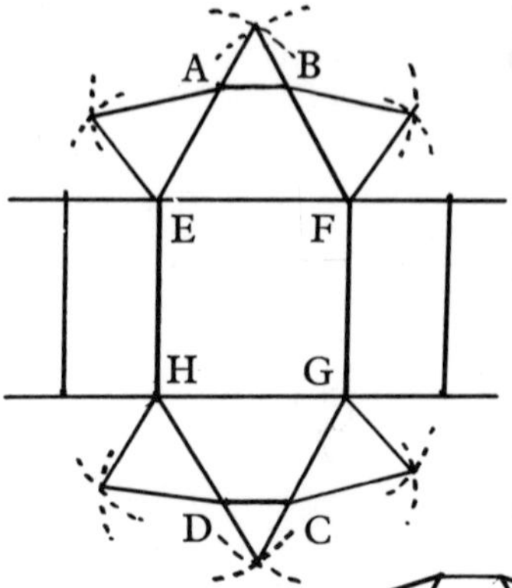

Make them out of thick paper. The central area EFGH is 1·5cm ($\frac{3}{4}$in) square and the sides 7·5mm ($\frac{1}{4}$in) wide. To get the slopes of roofs and brackets, strike arcs of 1·5cm ($\frac{3}{4}$in) from E, F, G and H. Join them up to form triangles and measure off in 1cm ($\frac{2}{5}$in) to find A, B, C and D. From these four points strike arcs of 1cm ($\frac{2}{5}$in) to cross arcs of 7mm ($\frac{1}{4}$in) from E, F, G and H. Now add flaps (black in diagram) and mark and cut out the windows. Back the windows with cellophane, fold the window and glue it in position.

Chimneys
Use strips of 5mm ($\frac{1}{4}$in) square balsa wood. For the chimney on end wall BC cut two lengths 11·5cm ($4\frac{1}{2}$in) and one 5cm ($2\frac{1}{2}$in) with a sloping top.

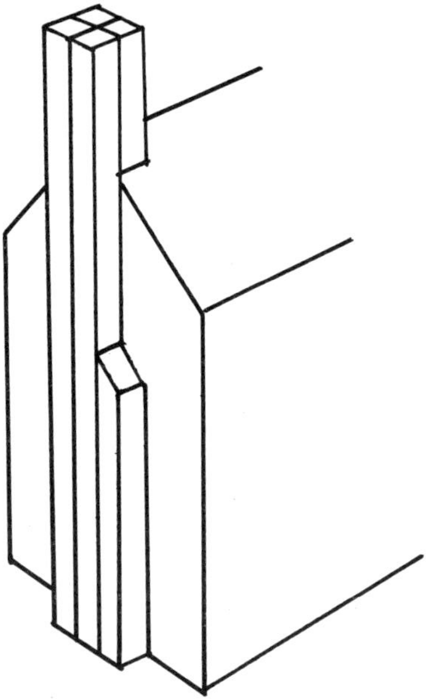

Glue these in position, then cut two short lengths to fit the slope of the roof, making the top of the chimney square. For the other two chimneys use 1cm ($\frac{1}{2}$in) balsa or four pieces of 5mm ($\frac{1}{4}$in). Cut the lower edges carefully to fit the slope of the roofs.

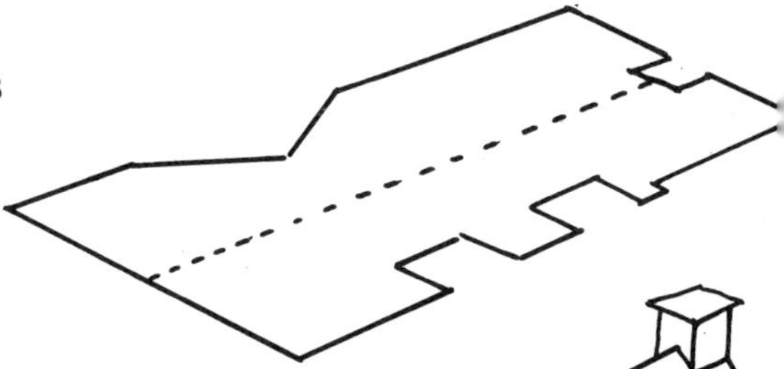

The tops of all three chimneys should be covered with a small square of card, slightly larger than the top.
NB. Do not glue the two small chimneys in position until roofs have been finished.

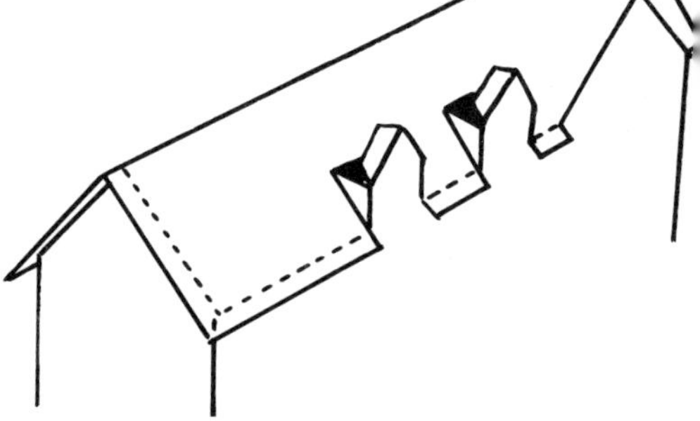

Roofs
For the roof of the main building cut a piece of card 21·5cm ($8\frac{1}{2}$in) by 10cm (4in). This will give overlap for the eaves. Fold it along the middle. Carefully mark the positions of the end chimney, gables and back wing. Cut the roof away behind the dormers to the line of the wall.

The roof on the back wing is very irregular in shape and you will have to try it out in paper first. Then trace it onto cardboard, cut it out and glue it in place.

The roofs for all the dormer windows should project as far as the main roofs. Again, work these out in paper first. The two small front ones will be as in diagram **a**, the two back ones as in diagram **b**, and the large front one as in diagram **c**. To attach them firmly, put a little glue along the back edges of the roofs as well as on the flaps.

a

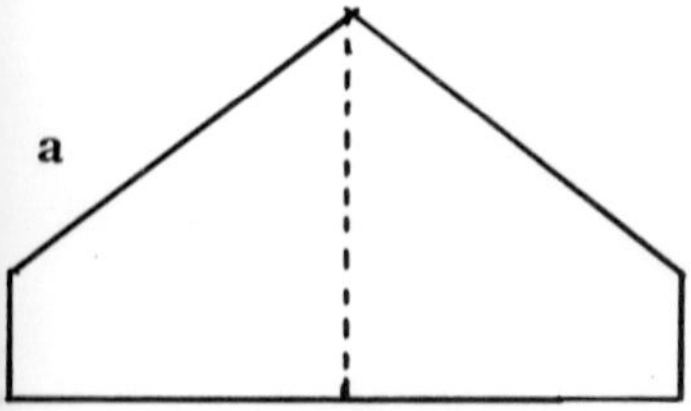

b

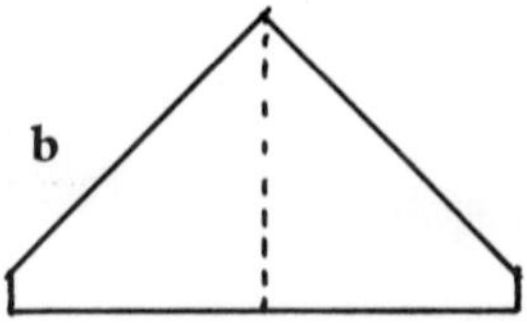

c

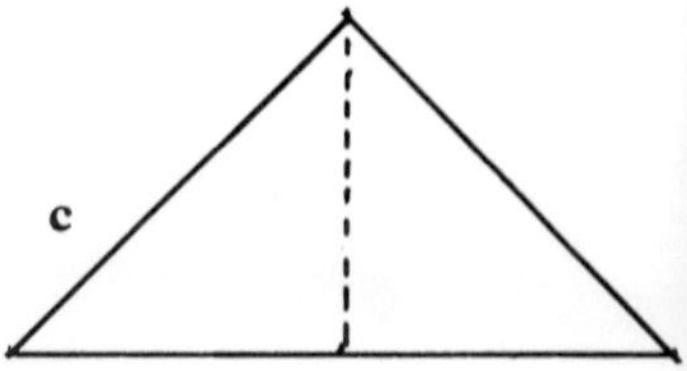

Painting (see colour charts pages 16–17)
Roof are of rusty-red tile.

Stone foundation walls and chimneys are very light stone – almost white. Use white, with a tiny amount of dark brown and blue.

The plasterwork is slightly darker in tone. Mix a tiny amount of yellow ochre with white.

Most of the timbering has recently been restored with new oak, which is a light, silvery-brown colour – much lighter than the dark brown old oak we usually associate with 'black-and-white' timbering. Mix white and yellow ochre in equal quantities with a little dark brown and blue.

The White House, Washington

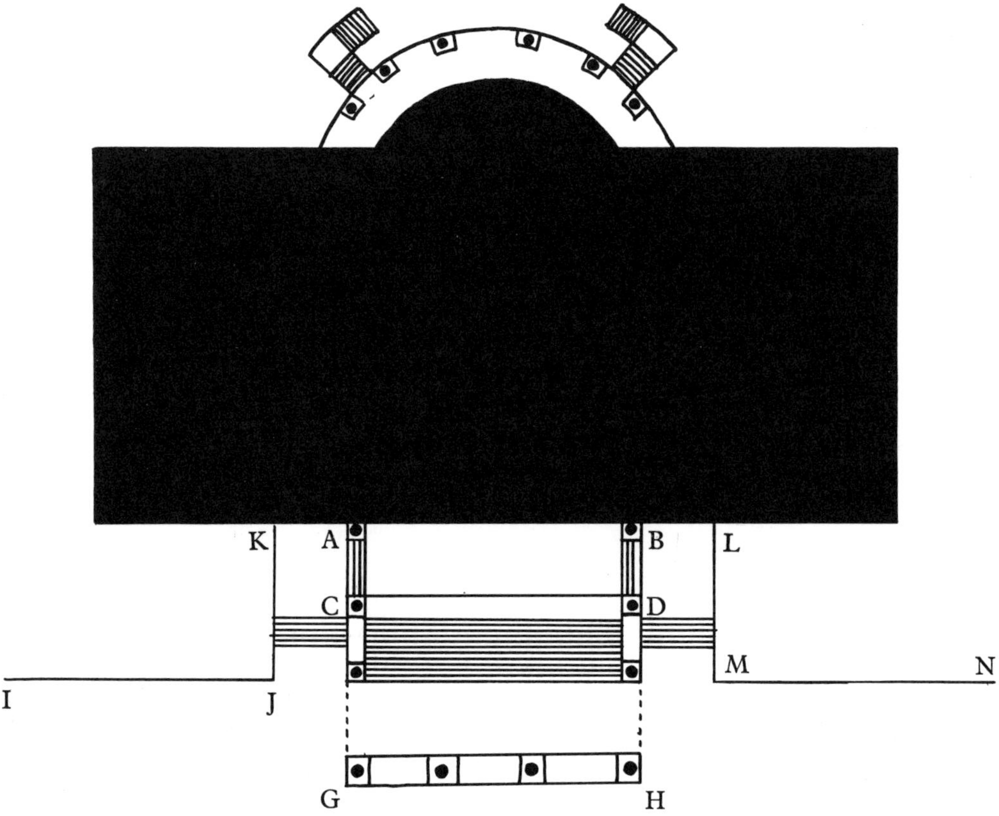

In sixteenth-century Italy the architect Palladio built elegant country houses with beautifully proportioned rooms and entrance porches like Roman temples. King James I's architect, Inigo Jones, took this style to England and, during the seventeenth and eighteenth centuries, hundreds of 'Palladian' mansions were built all over Britain and the United States. The most famous is the White House, which was begun in 1792. Many additions and alterations have been made to it since then. For this model we shall concentrate on the main block, shown as a ground plan below, leaving out the later single-storey buildings on both sides.

Draw a base line 1cm ($\frac{1}{2}$in) above the lower edge of the card. Rule a second line for the top of the wall 8·2cm ($3\frac{1}{4}$in) above the base. Measure AB 13cm (5in), BC (entrance front) 28cm (11in), CD 13cm (5in). Continue lines up from C and D 28cm (11in) for roof CDEF. Measure DG and EH 8·2cm ($3\frac{1}{4}$in) for the garden front.

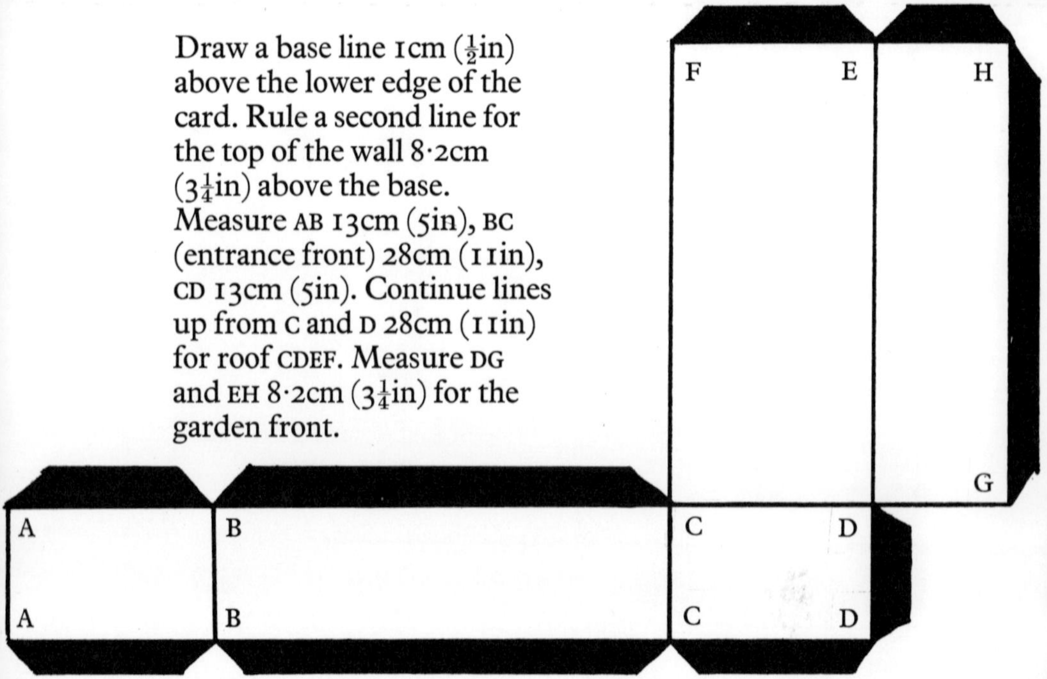

Add flaps (black in diagram).

Before cutting out, mark out the following heights for windows and floor levels between AA and DD, and also between DG and EH, starting from the base line: J 6mm ($\frac{1}{4}$in), K 6mm ($\frac{1}{4}$in), L 6mm ($\frac{1}{4}$in), M 6mm ($\frac{1}{4}$in), N 2cm ($\frac{3}{4}$in), O 12mm ($\frac{1}{2}$in), and P 12mm ($\frac{1}{2}$in).

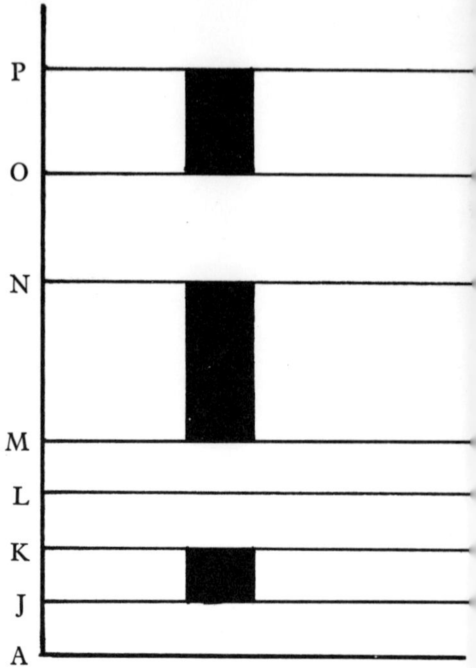

Sides AB and CD
Rule a line down the centre of each side and measure outwards from this line.

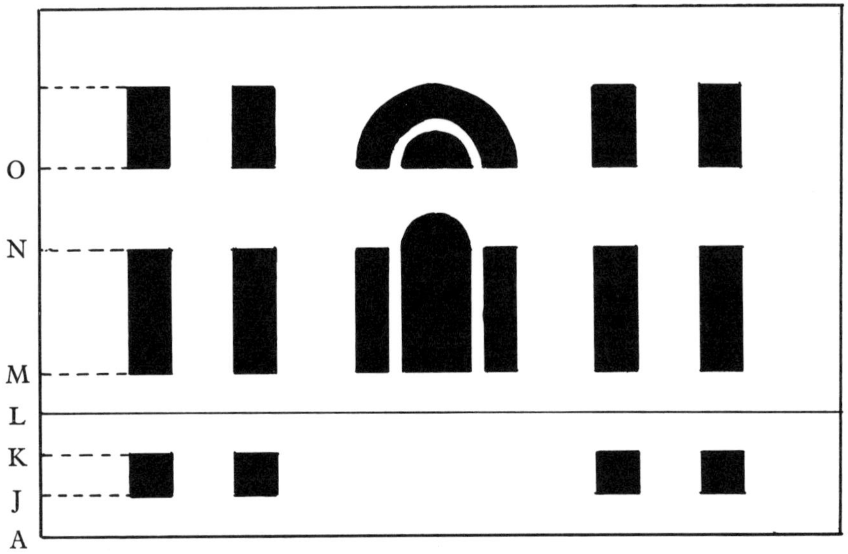

On line O mark out the round-arched window – a typical feature of Palladian buildings. Draw three semicircles with radii of 5mm ($\frac{1}{5}$in), 7mm ($\frac{3}{10}$in), and 12mm ($\frac{1}{2}$in). On line N mark out one semicircle, radius 5mm ($\frac{1}{5}$in). Carry ends of this semicircle straight down to line M. Mark out narrow windows on either side – 2mm ($\frac{1}{10}$in) for the window frame, 5mm ($\frac{1}{5}$in) for the window.

Mark out two windows on all three floors on each side. Starting from edge of central windows, measure: wall 15mm ($\frac{1}{2}$in), window 7mm ($\frac{1}{4}$in), wall 11mm ($\frac{2}{5}$in), window 7mm ($\frac{1}{4}$in).

Entrance front (BC)

Start by marking out WX 10cm (4in) for position of central entrance portico.

Starting at the left edge, B, measure: wall 12mm ($\frac{1}{2}$in) and window 7mm ($\frac{1}{4}$in) alternately until you reach W.

For the centre section WX (no basement windows) measure 15mm ($\frac{5}{8}$in), 7mm ($\frac{1}{4}$in), 25mm (1in), door 7mm ($\frac{1}{4}$in), 25mm (1in), 7mm ($\frac{1}{4}$in), 15mm ($\frac{5}{8}$in). Repeat these

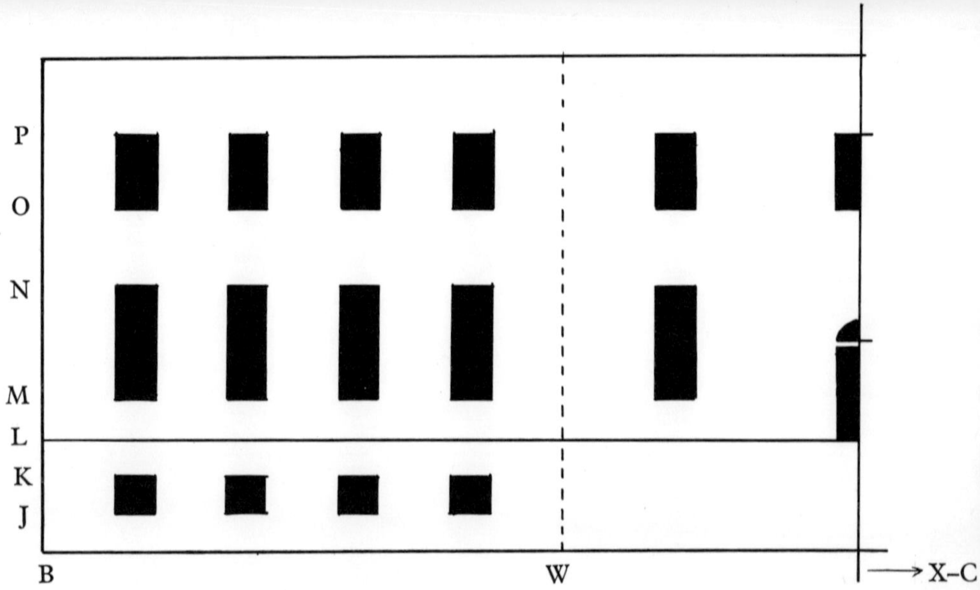

measurements between X and C as for BW but in reverse order.

Garden front (GH)

Mark out YZ 8cm (3in) for the curved centre section. Starting from the outside edges DG and EH, measure walls 12mm ($\frac{1}{2}$in) and windows 7mm ($\frac{1}{4}$in) alternately – five windows on each side of the centre section on all three floors.

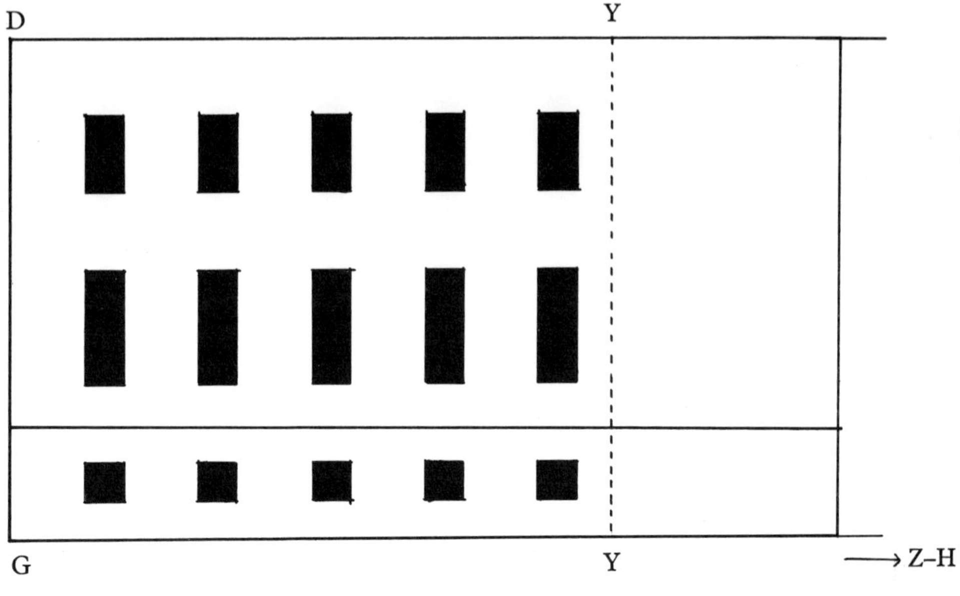

Cut out windows and doors on all four sides.

The two upper floors have quite large frames round the windows as you can see from the photograph of the side of the building. The lower edges are supported on pairs of stone brackets. These can be drawn on to the card but, if you have the patience, it will look much more real if you cut out frames from card. Make frames for the semi-circular side windows. Glue these frames in position before backing the windows with cellophane.

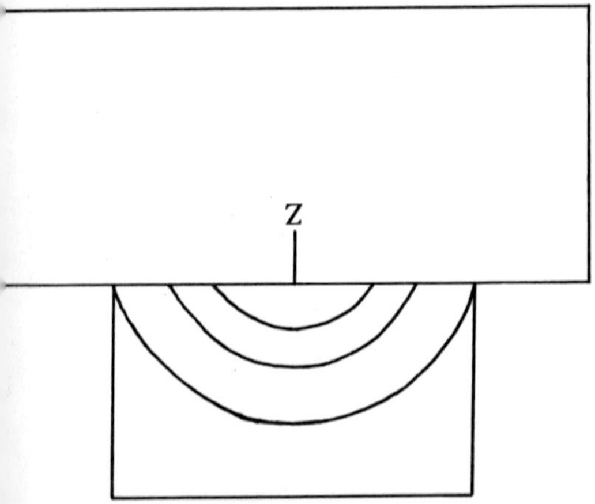

Base
Fold and glue the main building.

Make a base of card the exact size of the building. Include a terrace on the garden front 9 × 14cm ($3\frac{1}{2} \times 5\frac{1}{2}$in). To obtain curved lines for steps and terrace find the centre of the garden front and mark z 2·5cm (1in) inside the building. Then draw arcs of 4·5cm ($1\frac{3}{4}$in), 6cm ($2\frac{1}{2}$in), and 9cm ($3\frac{1}{2}$in).

Roof
Cut out a flat roof 2mm ($\frac{1}{10}$in) wider all round than the base. Mark out a curved projection the same way as for the base, with radii of 4·5cm ($1\frac{3}{4}$in) and 6cm ($2\frac{1}{2}$in). Attach the main building to the base and roof.

Cut out small blocks of balsa and glue them just inside the 6cm ($2\frac{1}{2}$in) curve under the roof and on top of the base.

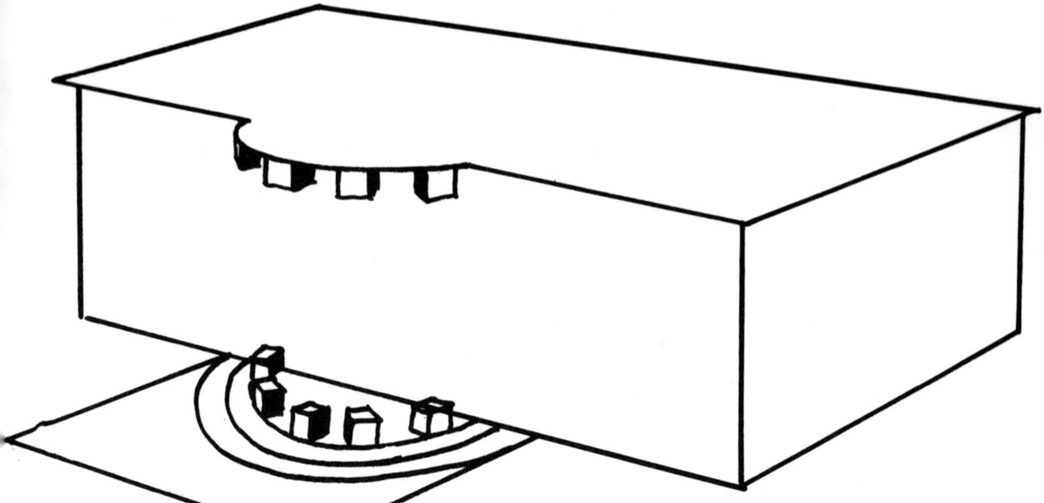

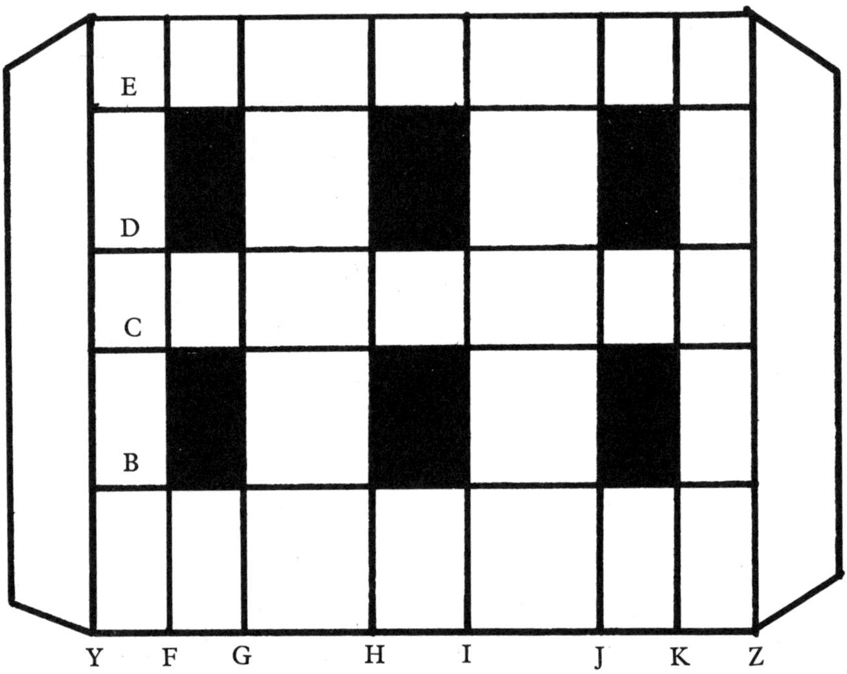

Curved (garden) front
Measure out the curved wall making YZ 8cm ($3\frac{1}{4}$in) high by 9cm ($3\frac{1}{2}$in) wide. Mark the door heights: YB 2cm ($\frac{3}{4}$in), BC 2cm ($\frac{3}{4}$in), CD 1·5cm ($\frac{1}{2}$in), DE 2cm ($\frac{3}{4}$in). Mark the widths: YF 1cm ($\frac{2}{5}$in), FG 1cm ($\frac{2}{5}$in), GH 2cm ($\frac{7}{10}$in), HI 1cm ($\frac{1}{2}$in), IJ 2cm ($\frac{7}{10}$in), JK 1cm ($\frac{2}{5}$in), KZ 1cm ($\frac{2}{5}$in).

Cut out the doors, back them with cellophane. Draw, score and fold the side flaps and cut out the wall. Glue one flap into position and allow it to dry before gluing the wall to the balsa blocks and then gluing the second flap in position. Cut out and glue on simple door frames for the upper floor only.

Curved terrace on main (middle) floor
Rule a line 11cm ($4\frac{1}{2}$in) long on a piece of card. Find the centre and draw vertically down 2·5cm (1in) to obtain X, the centre for arcs of 4·5cm ($1\frac{3}{4}$in) and 6cm ($2\frac{1}{2}$in). Add flaps 2cm ($\frac{3}{4}$in) wide at each end and small flaps round the inner and outer curves. Glue the terrace into position.

Curved wall on basement floor

Cut out a strip of card 18mm (¾in) high by 13·5cm (5¾in) wide. Measure AB 7mm (¼in), BC 7mm (½in), CD 32mm (1¼in), DE 7mm (¼in), EF 10mm (½in), FG 8mm (¼in). This is the door in the centre. Now repeat the measurements in reverse order, starting with 10mm (½in), 7mm (¼in), 32mm (1¼in), 7mm (¼in), 7mm (½in).

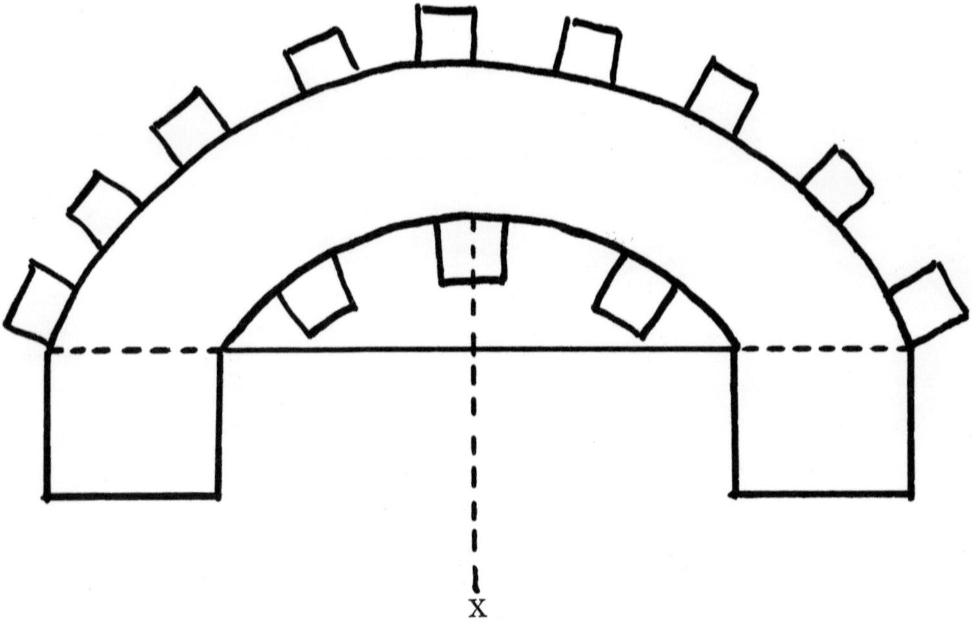

Cut out the doors and glue balsa strips on either side of them on the inside, to give thickness to the arches, and for gluing to the base.

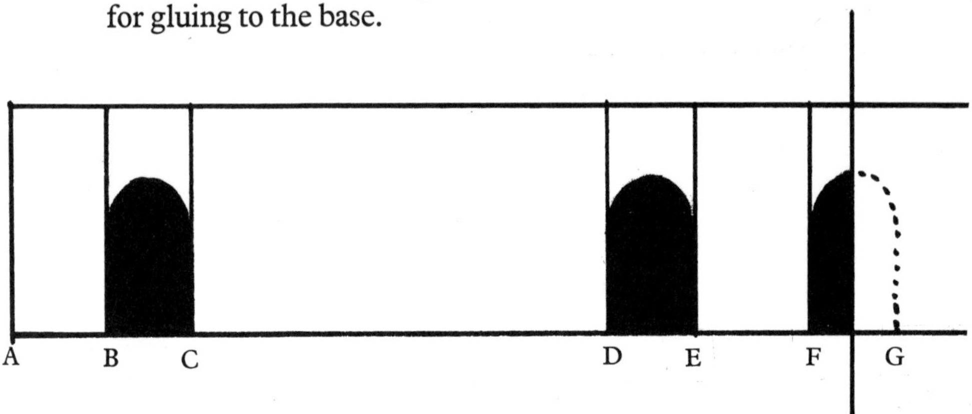

Pediments

All windows on the main (middle) floor have *pediments* – alternately triangular or segmental (curved). Cut a long strip of card 2·5mm ($\frac{1}{8}$in) wide. For the triangular pediments measure 12, 7, 7, 12mm ($\frac{1}{2}$, $\frac{5}{8}$, $\frac{5}{8}$, $\frac{1}{2}$in) score, fold and glue (see diagram).

For segmental pediments, measure 12, 14, 12mm ($\frac{1}{2}$, $\frac{5}{8}$, $\frac{1}{2}$in).

Glue them into position, just resting on top of the window frames.

Flat roof

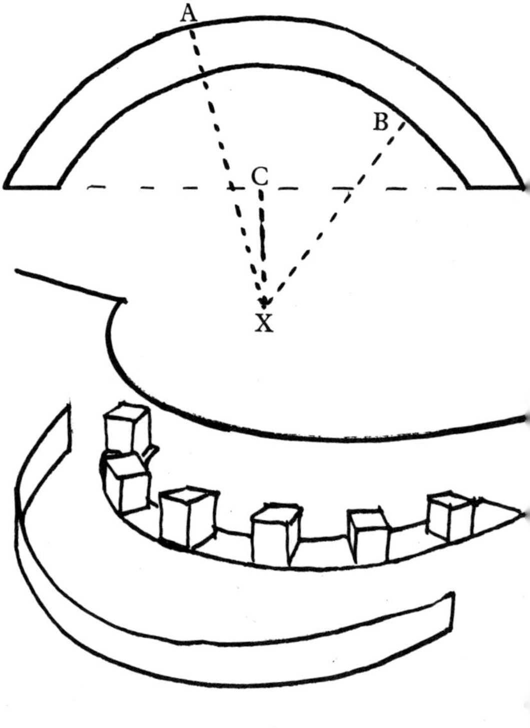

Mark out and glue on a second, flat roof, slightly larger all round than the first one (page 53).

Mark out a crescent shape to fit under the projecting curve of the roof, radii AX 6cm ($2\frac{1}{2}$in), BX 5cm (2in), CX 2·5cm (1in).

Glue small blocks of balsa along the edge of the card and glue this to the underside of the roof.

Glue a strip of card or paper round the front to hide the balsa blocks.

Upper floor balcony
In the same way cut out two crescents of card for the balcony of upper floor with radii of 4·5cm (1¾in) and 5cm (2in). Glue them together for strength and fix them in place. They should be level with the base of the upper floor windows. Then cut a strip of card 5mm (¼in) wide for the balcony railing.

Pillars
Cut small squares of balsa for the bases of the pillars and glue them onto the edge of the curved terrace on the main floor (see plan page 48).

Cut lengths of straw for pillars.

For the *Ionic capitals*, cut lengths of paper 5mm (⅛in) wide, 10cm (4in) long. Roll the ends towards the middle and, when they are the width of the straw apart, fix them with a spot of glue. Then glue each pillar to its base, and the capital under the roof.

a

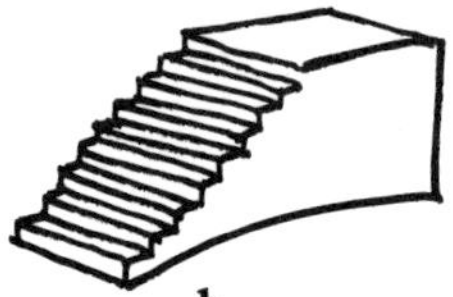

b

c

d

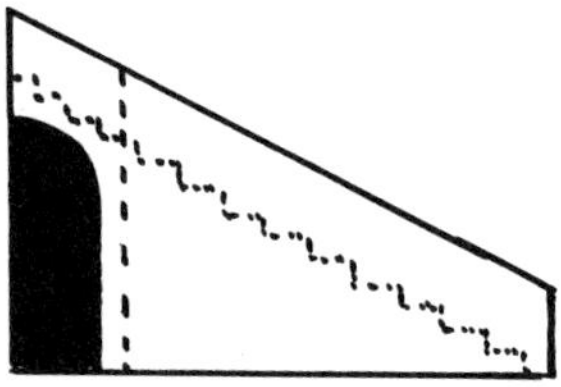

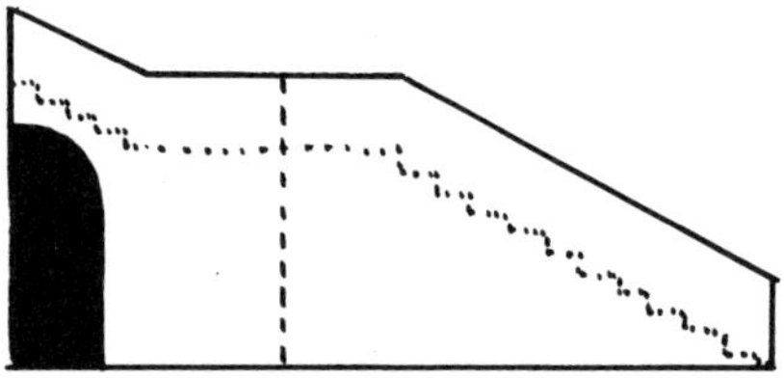

e

Curved stairways

Cut out a ring of card with radii of 7·5 and 8cm (3 and $3\frac{1}{4}$in). Cut out a segment of the ring long enough to act as the base of curved stairs (see plan on page 48 for the position and size). Keep cutting and gluing on shorter and shorter segments, **a**, until the top is square, **b**. Glue the staircase to the base with the square top opposite the space between two pillars nearest the main building. Add steps up to the terrace by overlapping rectangular pieces, **c**. Cut card to form sides and balustrades for both sides of the steps. Diagram **d** shows the shape for the inner balustrade and **e** for the outer one.

Repeat the reverse way round for other staircase.

Moulding

Cut a long strip of card 7·5mm ($\frac{1}{4}$in) wide and glue all round the walls of the building just beneath the roof ledge.

Cut another strip 18mm ($\frac{3}{4}$in) wide. Before gluing it round the base, cut out windows to correspond with the basement windows in the building.

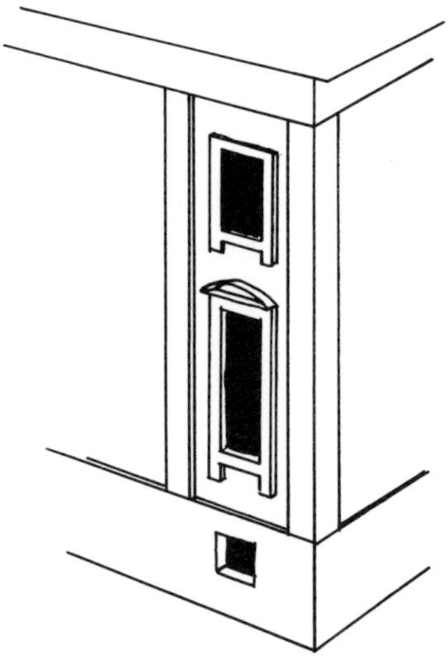

Cut out *pilasters* (flat pillars) 3mm ($\frac{1}{5}$in) wide and glue them between all the windows on all sides except the entrance front. Use double widths, folded, on corners of the building.

Roof

Trace round the roof onto a piece of card, adding 2mm ($\frac{1}{8}$in) all round and a projecting rectangle of 8·5 × 10cm ($3\frac{1}{2}$ × 4in) for the portico roof. Glue it in place and glue strips of square balsa wood 5mm ($\frac{1}{4}$in) wide all round under the portico roof.

Terrace

Mark out the floor of terrace ABCD 10 × 3·5cm (4 × $1\frac{1}{2}$in). AE, EF, GH, HC, BI, IJ, KL and LD should all measure 1cm ($\frac{2}{5}$in). FG, JK and all the sides of the platform should measure 1·5cm ($\frac{3}{5}$in).

Fold along the dotted lines, and cut all other lines. Glue the terrace to the base. Build up the two lower landings on each side by cutting rectangles of card 3·5 × 2·5cm ($1\frac{1}{2}$ × 1in) and raising them on balsa strips to 5mm ($\frac{1}{5}$in).

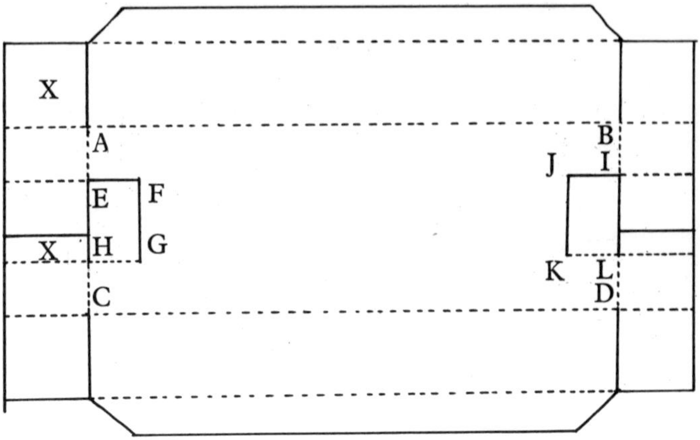

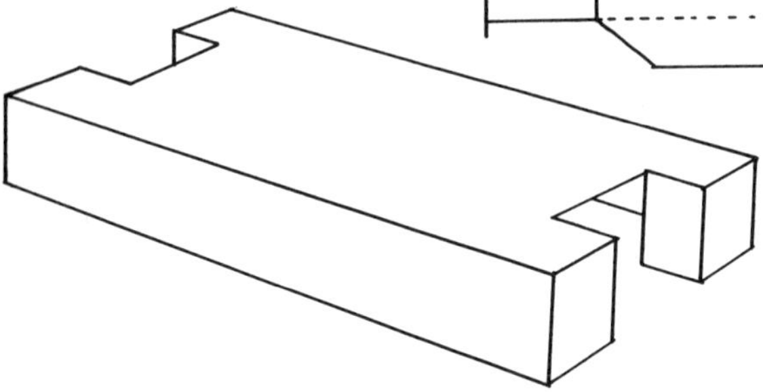

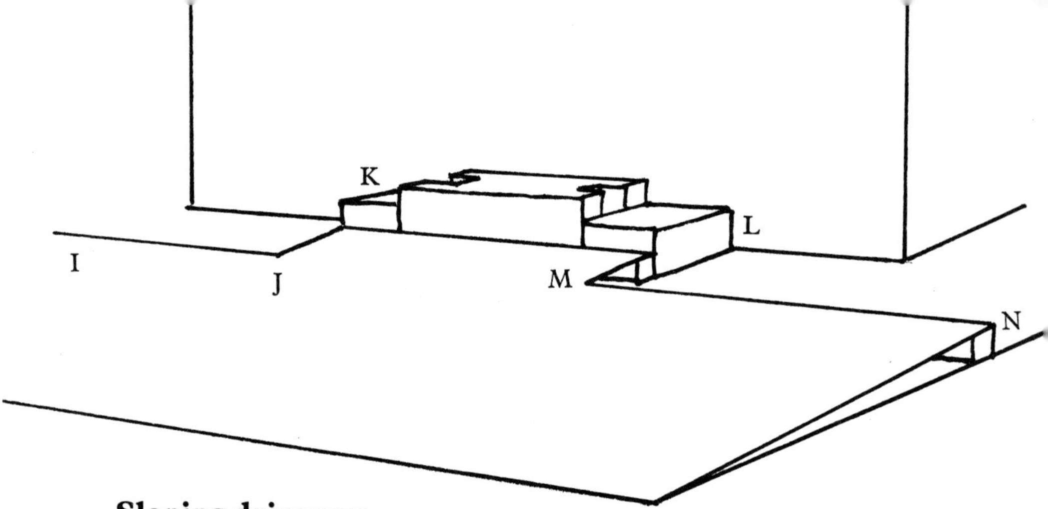

Sloping driveway

The ground slopes away from the front entrance of the White House. Cut a sheet of card the full width of your hardboard base, with a projection, JM, 1·5cm (½in) deep to coincide with the full width of the entrance steps.

Glue balsa strips to the underside from I to N and at the back of the projection. Glue it to the base board. Glue blocks of balsa, level with main terrace, on both sides of main steps. They should also form a low wall (GH on the plan on page 48) which supports the four main pillars of the portico.

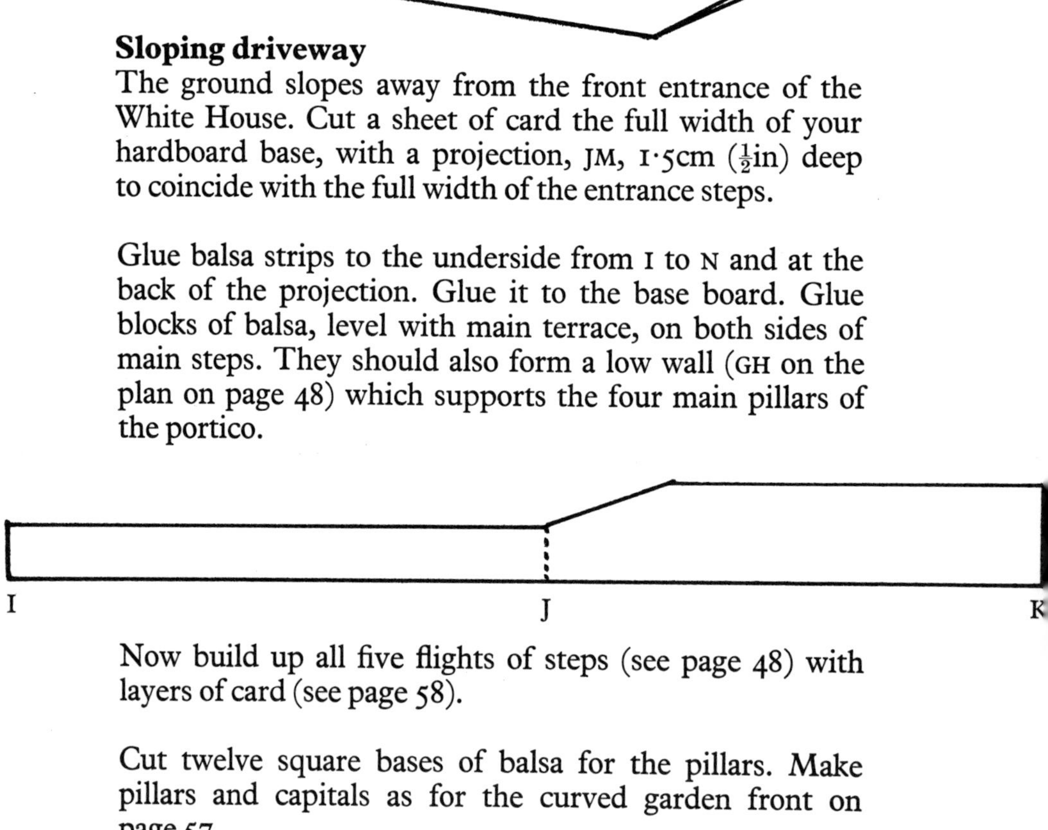

Now build up all five flights of steps (see page 48) with layers of card (see page 58).

Cut twelve square bases of balsa for the pillars. Make pillars and capitals as for the curved garden front on page 57.

Cut long strips of card IJK to make low walls along the outer steps and driveway. Repeat, in reverse, for LMN.

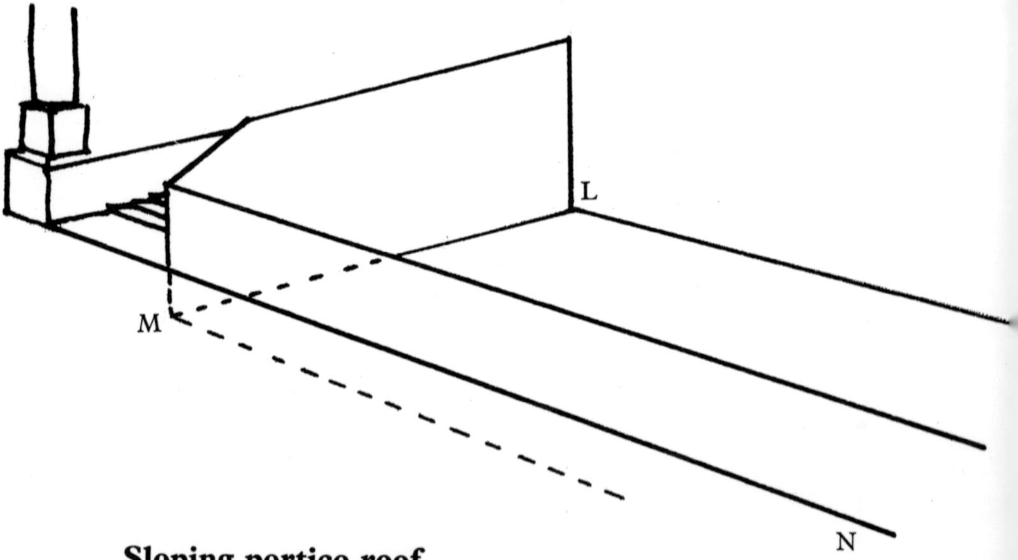

Sloping portico roof

Draw this out on thick paper AB, CD, EF are 8cm ($3\frac{1}{4}$in), AC, CE, BD, DF 6cm ($2\frac{1}{4}$in). Find G and H by striking arcs of 6cm ($2\frac{1}{4}$in) from C and D, and of 11cm ($4\frac{1}{5}$in) from E and F. Add flaps, and glue the roof onto the portico 2mm ($\frac{1}{10}$in) back from front edge. Cut a strip of card 1·5cm ($\frac{1}{2}$in) wide and 12cm ($4\frac{1}{2}$in) long. Fold it across the middle and glue it over the outer end of the portico roof, projecting 2mm ($\frac{1}{10}$in) beyond the front edge.

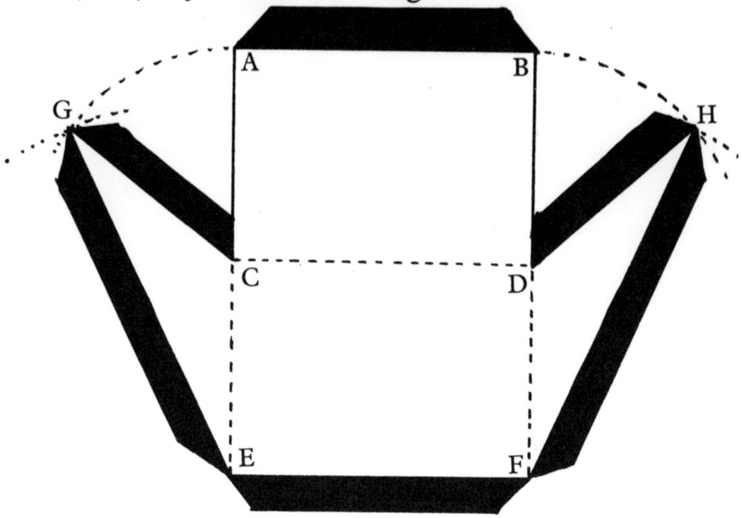

Parapet wall

There is a high *parapet* wall all round the outer edge of the roofs. Build it up with two thicknesses of 5mm ($\frac{1}{4}$in) balsa one on top of the other. Then, on the third layer, glue on short lengths of balsa to correspond with the corners of building, spaces between the windows, and above the pillars. Glue a thin strip of card all the way round on top. The parapets should be vertically in line with the main walls of the building and not on the outer edge of the roof, which juts out slightly.

Painting

Paint the whole building white, except for roofs and roads, which should be very pale grey.

Making a garden or landscape setting

You can see from the photographs in this book how the addition of trees, shrubs, hedges and uneven ground can give realism to an architectural model.

Trees

Make a trunk and branches from 15-or 30-amp fuse wire. Cut ten or more lengths. Most trees should be equal in height to a three-storey building. Twist all the strands together for about a third of their length, then begin to spread and separate them. Study real trees such as oak, elm and pine, and try to copy the arrangement of their branches. Coat the wires with glue or paste and wind tissue paper round them to hide the wires and provide an ideal painting surface. For foliage use lichen (sold at aero-model stores), or scraps of sponge, foam rubber, or felt.

Bore holes in the base for planting the trees and build up papier-maché round the base of the trunk to make it firm. (Papier-maché is simply scraps of newspaper or tissue soaked in water and mixed with paste.)

Hedges

For shrubs and bushes use same materials as for foliage. For small hedges cut strips of carpet or underfelt with a craft knife. For larger hedges use balsa wood covered with felt, baize or any rough-textured material.

Flower beds, etc.

Earth, flower-beds, rockeries and any uneven ground can be modelled into shape using papier-maché. Real pebbles and stone chips can be used as well.

How to start a model of your own

When you have made all the models in this book you should be able to make almost any type of house – old or new, large or small, from a log cabin to a palace. You will also be able to build a group of buildings like a school or small town.

In the planning stage it makes a big difference if you can actually visit the building and make your own plans and measurements. Otherwise you will have to work from plans and pictures in a book. There are several books which specialise in plans and elevations of famous buildings. Banister Fletcher's *History of Architecture* is still the best known and most complete. Many 'stately homes' and castles sell guide books, illustrated with plans and views. But, if you are going to measure a building yourself, this is how you should do it.

First, walk all round the building and draw a simple ground plan of its general shape. Then put in any projections – wings, buttresses, chimneys, porches, bay windows, etc. Next, mark in all the windows and doors.

Instead of trying to measure the whole length of each side at one go, measure the separate units one at a time – corner to first window, width of window, space to next window, and so on. If the building is symmetrical, you will only need to measure one window and one wall space

Now draw an elevation (side view) of all four walls, showing doors, windows, balconies, parapets, roofs and all mouldings, ornaments, etc. Measuring the heights of these is more difficult, unless you know how to do trigonometry, but it is possible to estimate heights in other ways.

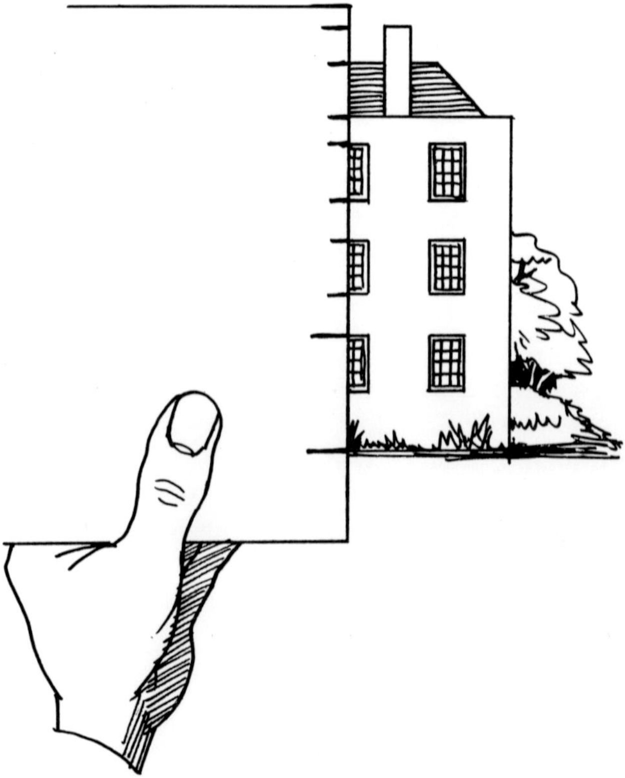

If the walls are of brick or even-sized stones, measure the height of one brick or stone and multiply by the number of rows. Count the number of rows up to the tops and bottoms of the windows.

If this method is not possible, measure the distance from the ground to the top of the first line of windows, or some other feature that you can reach. Then, standing a good distance (at least thirty paces) away, hold out a piece of stiff paper or card, vertically, at arm's length. Make pencil marks on the edge of the paper at ground level and at the point you have previously measured. Then mark in all the other heights you require. You can then estimate fairly accurately the actual measurements of the building.

When you have collected all the necessary measurements you must decide on the scale of your model. 1cm=1m ($\frac{1}{10}$in=1ft) are easy scales to work with, but the size of your building may compel you to work with a larger or smaller scale.

Next, draw a rough sketch of the building as it would look from the air. This will help you to decide its basic shape and how best to construct it. Work out in rough how you can fit as many walls and roofs as possible together onto one piece of card – the method used in this book. When you have done this, draw out the whole thing to the correct scale on paper. Do not bother with doors and windows and other details at this stage. Cut it out, fold it, and see if it works. You will probably find that you have to make some alterations, add some flaps, change the slope of a roof, etc. When it is correct, copy it out onto cardboard and the most difficult part is over!

Glossary

battlements A low wall, round the edge of a roof, with wide notches in the top. Usually found on castles and other fortifications.

buttresses Props of wood, stone or brick built against a wall to strengthen it.

capital The upper, decorated part of a column or pillar.

cloister A covered walk enclosing a quadrangle. Usually found in monasteries and cathedrals.

dormer window Usually a bedroom or attic window that sticks out vertically from a sloping roof.

gable The upper part of an end wall of a house, usually pointed at the top with a ridged roof over it. A gabled window has this same ridged or pointed roof over it.

Ionic A kind of Greek architecture in which the pillars were decorated at the top with a scroll-shaped ornament.

lintel A horizontal beam of wood or stone over a doorway or opening.

oriel window A bay window built out from a wall and resting not on the ground but on a support.

parapet A low wall round the edge of a roof. Often found on fortifications.

pediment A broad triangular part, usually of stone, above an entrance or doorway.

pilaster A rectangular column, with a capital and a base, built into a wall.

portico Usually a porch; but also an open space with a roof held up by columns.

solar A balcony or room exposed to the sun.

Index